GROWING UP TO BE A CHILD

A Paediatrician Explores Jesus' Invitation
to 'Become Like a Little Child'

T0147244

PETER SIDEBOTHAM

WESTBOW
PRESS
A DIVISION OF THOMAS NELSON
& ZONDERVAN

Scripture quotations taken from
The Holy Bible, New International Version (Anglicised edition)
Copyright ©1979, 1984, 2011 by Biblica (formerly International Bible Society).
Used by permission of Hodder & Stoughton Publishers,
an Hachette UK company.
All rights reserved.
'NIV' is a registered trademark of Biblica (formerly International Bible Society).
UK trademark number 1448790.

WestBow Press books may be ordered through booksellers or by contacting:

WestBow Press
A Division of Thomas Nelson & Zondervan
1663 Liberty Drive
Bloomington, IN 47403
www.westbowpress.com
1 (866) 928-1240

ISBN: 978-1-4908-4067-3 (sc)
ISBN: 978-1-4908-4068-0 (hc)
ISBN: 978-1-4908-4066-6 (e)

Library of Congress Control Number: 2014910774

Printed in the United States of America.

WestBow Press rev. date: 7/25/2014

PREFACE

In August 2011, my daughter Esther, then nineteen, left home to work for a year in industry before going on to university to study engineering. That was just one of a number of major life events which occurred in quick succession, each of which had a profound impact on my life.

I was surprised at how much Esther's departure affected me. As a father, I had watched her grow and develop over those nineteen years. Now, here she was, no longer the little baby I had helped bring into the world, loved, and nurtured, but a beautiful, fully grown adult, launching out on her own journey of life.

In the preceding months, as I started to think about her leaving, I decided to write down my thoughts in a book for her – perhaps the greatest gift I could give her on her leaving. In doing so, I reflected on all I had learned from her and her brother, Joseph, about what it means to be a parent. I was privileged in this to be able to draw on my twenty-plus years of experience as a paediatrician, watching children grow and develop, and learning, too, from them and their parents.

My starting point, and what I most wanted to pass on to my daughter, was an exploration of what Jesus meant when he said, 'Unless you change and become like little children, you will never enter the kingdom of heaven.'[1] For me, both my life as a parent and

---

[1]   Matthew 18:3.

my life as a paediatrician were intrinsically bound up in my journey of faith. As I reflected on this, I began to realise just how much might be packed within that simple statement of Jesus's. Likewise, Jesus's words to Nicodemus, 'No one can see the kingdom of God unless he is born again', seemed to capture so much more than our typical evangelical interpretation.

So this book, drawing on my experience as a parent, a paediatrician, and a would-be follower of Jesus, seeks to explore what it might mean to truly be born again and become like a little child.

In publishing this book and making it available to a wider audience, I was confronted with a dilemma – how to balance the very personal and intimate nature of a gift to my daughter with something that could be accessible and meaningful for others.

I decided to keep the personal touch. That, after all, is where the book sprang from. I hope that you, my reader, will bear with me in that, and that you will find the way the book is addressed to Esther, and my frequent indulgence in expressing my feelings towards her, will somehow add to, rather than detract from, what you are able to get from your reading.

Above all, I hope that you may also grasp something of the magnitude of God's love for you – a love that is so much greater than any human father's love for his daughter. You too, dear reader, are God's beloved child.

I write this book as a white, professional male and a father. That is what I am, and I am content to be so. I am aware, however, that this brings its dangers, particularly with respect to the diversity of nature and culture that makes up humankind, and in the language and images we use to portray God.

Where I describe a child's development, and particularly where I write directly to Esther, I have tended to refer to a father and a daughter. In referring to God, I have tried, where possible, to use gender-neutral language. In order to avoid cumbersome and messy use of pronouns, however, I have at times resorted to the use of the masculine pronoun.

Apart from some of the Psalms, for which I have turned to Jim Cotter's excellent interpretation, *Psalms for a pilgrim people*,[2] I have used the New International Version of the Bible throughout. That is the version with which I am most familiar. I recognise, however, that this translation tends to resort to the masculine in reference to God. I apologise to any who find this uncomfortable.

Having said that, there is one aspect in which I think the use of the masculine to refer to God carries something profoundly important. Jesus himself referred to God exclusively as 'Abba', 'Father', and encouraged us to do the same. While there are many examples in the Bible of a feminine, motherly portrayal of God, I think that Jesus's use of 'Father' conveys something deeply significant about God.

Jesus came to show us the way to the Father, to reveal God to us as the true, loving Father. Many people will find that difficult, particularly because their own experiences of human fathers have been so flawed. This may particularly be so for those who have been abused physically, emotionally or sexually by their fathers or father-figures, or those whose fathers have been absent, whether physically or emotionally. Perhaps what is needed is not to discard the concept of God as a loving Father, but to see, in the way Jesus revealed God, what a true father is like. I hope that something of this will come through in the pages of this book.

---

[2]   J. Cotter. *Psalms for a pilgrim people.* New York: Morehouse Publishing, 1998.

Two other life events have never been far from my mind as I have worked on revising this book for publication. The first, at about the same time as my daughter's departure, was a long-distance cycle ride. In 2011, my son, Joe, then sixteen, rode 1,200 miles across the length of Britain, from Land's End to John O'Groats, on a unicycle.[3] I set out to accompany him on a bicycle, but through an unexpected illness was unable to complete the ride. Nevertheless, I gained an incredible amount through the months of training that preceded the ride, and the time I was able to spend with Joe. I remain indebted to Joe, alongside Esther, for teaching me what it means to be a parent.

The second event was the sudden, unexpected death of my wife, and Esther and Joe's mother, Helen, in January 2012. It is to Helen that I owe the biggest debt of gratitude: for her love for me over twenty-four wonderful years of marriage; for her support through the long, hard years of training to become a paediatrician; and, most of all, for being the incredible mother she was to our children. Esther and Joe would not be the young people they have grown to become without her unfailing love and commitment to them.

There are many people whom I want to thank, who have helped me in developing this book and in supporting me and caring for me in the life journey that has informed my thinking. I have been immensely privileged to have two wonderful, supportive parents, who have given me a tremendous inheritance of life and faith. I am profoundly grateful to the many friends who have encouraged me to get the book published, and have offered feedback and advice as I have redrafted it. Above all, I am grateful to my son, Joe; to Helen; and to Esther, for whom this book was written.

---

[3]   This unicycle ride is described in P. Sidebotham and J. Sidebotham. *The unicyclist, the vicar and the paediatrician.* Kibworth Beauchamp, UK: Matador, 2013.

A letter to my daughter

Dear Esther,

Last year I wrote a book with and for your brother.[4] This, as you know, was sparked off by his decision to ride from Coventry to Bristol on a unicycle, with me accompanying him. One day and one hundred (or so) miles later, I had learned a bit about Joseph, and a bit more about myself. It got me thinking. I had lived with Joseph for fifteen years, and yet it took something extraordinary to inspire me to write. Similarly, I have lived with you for nearly nineteen years. We may not have done anything as extraordinary as a long-distance unicycle ride, but you and I have been together a long time, and yes, you have inspired me – you've inspired me to rise to the challenge of being a father, to think and reflect, and now to write some of that down.

Although it had always been one of my dreams, I set out on this incredible journey nineteen years ago really knowing very little about what it means to be a father and to bring up children. Over these years, I have learned from you. And not just about how to be a father. I have learned about what it means to grow up.

In one of the most extraordinary statements of all time, Jesus, taking a little child, told his disciples, 'Unless you change and become like little children, you will never enter the kingdom of heaven.'[5] On another occasion, when the disciples were trying to stop little children coming to him, Jesus said, 'Let the little children come to me, and do not hinder them, for the kingdom of heaven belongs to such as these.'[6] And 'Anyone who will not receive the kingdom of God like a little child will never enter it.'[7]

---

4   P. Sidebotham and J. Sidebotham. *The unicyclist, the vicar and the paediatrician.* Kibworth Beauchamp, UK: Matador, 2013.
5   Matthew 18:3.
6   Matthew 18:14.
7   Mark 10:15.

Then, in an even more outrageous statement, Jesus told Nicodemus, a sensible, intelligent member of the Jewish ruling council, 'No-one can see the kingdom of God unless he is born again.'[8] Although that particular verse is often bandied about and used, in a rather narrow way, by evangelical Christians as a kind of badge to distinguish those who are 'in' from those who are 'out' of God's kingdom, I wonder whether Nicodemus was actually a bit closer to the truth when he asked Jesus, 'How can a man be born when he is old? Surely he cannot enter a second time into his mother's womb to be born!'[9]

Jesus didn't reprimand him or call him stupid for asking that question. Rather, it was almost as if he intended his statement to stimulate such an incredulous response. True, Jesus went on to speak of being 'born of water and the Spirit',[10] but he didn't retract his original statement. Perhaps we have been too quick to explain this away in spiritual terms, without really exploring the full impact of what it might mean to be 'born again' or to 'become like a little child'.

In my work I have seen thousands of babies and children, each of whom has perhaps taught me something of what this means. I have had the joy of seeing babies come into the world, take their first breaths, and make their first attempts to communicate with the world. I have had the opportunity to study child development, to observe what happens as a child grows, and to agonise over how and why it sometimes seems to go wrong. I have learned from these children and their families.

But most of all, I have learned from you: helping, nineteen years ago, to bring you into the world; watching you grow; observing with wonder and pride as you have grown into a wonderful young woman.

At the same time, I have thought about what it means to follow Jesus. I have tried to grapple with his teaching and what that means for me. And also what it might mean for you, a young woman leaving home and starting a new phase of your life.

---

8   John 3:3.
9   John 3:4.
10 John 3:5.

So this book is for you. Through its pages I will try to explore what that all means. Perhaps, in a small way, this can give back something of all I have learned and gained from you – my wonderful, precious daughter.

Your loving father.

August 2011

1

SOURCE

You knit me together in my mother's womb.

- Psalm 139:13

Being born must be an incredibly traumatic experience. The poor baby girl, after nine months cocooned in a warm, moist, quiet, and dark nest, is suddenly squeezed and pushed through a narrow hole. Her head is compressed much as a towel when put through a mangle, only to emerge into a cold, noisy, frightening new environment. It is hardly any wonder the first thing most babies do is cry.

It is traumatic for the father too. We are, of course, much maligned by mothers, who think they have the worst of the deal. I don't want to minimise the pain mothers go through, but it's not easy for the fathers either. Often we have been dragged out of bed at an unearthly hour, only to have to wait around before anything happens. We have to remain strong and cheerful while being shouted at and having our knuckles crushed. All the while we have no control over events. After the baby is born, everyone asks how the baby and the mother are; no one seems interested in how the father is.

Why childbirth is so painful is a mystery. From a purely anatomical point of view, there seem to be two key issues. First, the baby's head is big. That is important because of the size and sensitivity of our brains. In comparison to other animals, the human brain is inordinately large. Yet it seems we hardly use any of its capacity, and we certainly have a very limited understanding of how it works. Our brains are amazing, though, and an integral part of what it means to be human.

The second point is that the mother's pelvis is relatively small. This, also, is important, as it is the narrowness of the pelvis that allows the mother (and fathers too for that matter) to stand upright and move on two feet. This is another integral part of being human.

So we have the problem of a bipedal, thinking organism producing another bipedal, thinking organism, and the two don't really match. However, all is not lost. Our skulls have been made with a number of interlocking bones, which in the adult are fused together and hard but in a newborn infant are still separate, soft, and pliable. During delivery, the baby's head can mould, allowing it to squeeze through the birth canal while still providing protection to the sensitive brain within. It is quite amazing that babies almost universally survive this process without damage to the brain.

However, I wonder whether there is something more than just an anatomical reason for the trauma of childbirth. The Bible seems to suggest there is, locating it right at the heart of the consequences of the fall, when the Lord God says to the woman, 'I will greatly increase your pains in childbearing; with pain you will give birth to children.'[11] That was the consequence of eating from the tree of the knowledge of good and evil. It is interesting how that ties in with the anatomical issues above, with the development of the human brain being one of the prime reasons why there is the mismatch.

But why should that be the curse on the woman? True, the man gets his curse as well, having to work in painful toil to eat. But why

---

[11] Genesis 1:16.

painful childbirth for the woman? Perhaps it is somehow related to the deeper mystery of the pain of relationship, or of the bonding between a mother and her child. I don't know, and I think this may remain a mystery.

You, dear Esther, I, and each person living on this earth were born through their mothers' pain. Life is not cheap – not anyone's life. Perhaps that is part of the mystery. If a mother can go through that pain to deliver her baby, that baby must be worth the pain – and so much more. And you, my wonderful daughter – you were worth every bit of the struggle I had to endure. And I know, though my struggle pales into insignificance beside hers, your mother would have said, even more, that you were worth it.

Childbirth may be painful, but it is also amazing. The first time I ever witnessed a baby being born was as a medical student on my obstetric attachment. I had arranged to do part of my attachment at our local hospital. At the time, they didn't have any regular medical students, so the midwives – mostly big, buxom West Indians – took me under their wings and determined that I should get as much out of this as possible.

On my first day, one of the midwives swept me into the nearest delivery room, introduced me to a labouring mother, and told me to put a pair of gloves on. Then, with the mother pushing, panting, and sweating, the father pushing, panting, and sweating beside her, and me pushing, panting, and sweating even more at the other end, between us we produced an amazing little baby.

I'm sure I cried as much as both the parents as the head squeezed out, followed immediately by a tiny, pink body. It was such a privilege to witness and be part of. I went on to deliver dozens of babies over those few weeks, and the experience of that obstetric attachment was one of the most incredible things I have ever done.

But that, my dear Esther, was nothing compared to the wonder of your birth: to help ease you out into the world, watch you fill your lungs and let out your first cry, cut the cord that had kept you alive those nine months, and pass you up to your mum, knowing that you were my daughter. Those were emotions that will stay with me forever. You were, and still are, my beloved daughter. We were starting out on an incredible journey together. You may have been slimy, wrinkled, and squashed; you may have greeted us with nothing more than a cry; but you were ours.

Preparation

Dramatic as it may be, birth is not the beginning. First there is a miraculous fusion of two living cells, followed by the nine months of gestation that precede a birth. It is an amazing period of what, to me, seems like almost constant miracles. Somehow, that one fused cell, drawing on information contained in microscopic strands of DNA, manages to divide into two, four, eight, sixteen, and eventually billions of cells, all different in their structures and functions. As they divide, those cells organise themselves into different organs and tissues, aligning and connecting with each other in the most incredible, choreographed dance. And all this is unseen.

Long before you were born, you were perfectly formed as a tiny human being – not just your little hands and feet, but your eyes and ears, liver and kidneys, nervous system, endocrine pathways, and circulation, all ticking over, getting ready for life in the outside world, and joining in that dance. And what is equally incredible, your body was not just getting ready for living in the world but simultaneously coping with living in the protected environment of your mother's womb. So you had two systems developing side by side – taking oxygen, energy, and nutrients from, and getting rid of carbon dioxide and other waste products to your mother, while preparing to suddenly switch your circulation, digestion, and elimination functions within moments of your birth.

While you, my treasure, were beavering away inside, growing and developing and preparing yourself for the great day, your mother too was working hard to ensure you could do so, and to prepare both of you for the momentous event of your birth. She had to eat enough for you both, keep breathing, exercising, and eliminating (even more than usual as you were helpfully pressing on her bladder), avoid things that might be harmful to you, go for health check-ups and scans, and prepare her body for the Herculean ordeal she was going to face.

As a father, I too chipped in – supporting your mum, coping with her heightened emotions, being a good father-to-be. And both of us were busy getting ready in other ways – begging, borrowing, and buying baby equipment, clearing out and decorating a room to be your nursery, and wondering what it would be like to be parents.

No birth comes easily. It follows months of careful preparation with a lot of investment, certainly on the part of the parents, but from others too – family and friends, the midwives and obstetrician. And then, of course, there is all the natural preparation, to which we contribute very little other than attempting to provide the best environment for it to happen. The miracle of new birth is not so much the birth itself, but all that has gone before. In a sense, though, that is only the end of the beginning. The whole of the rest of your life lay ahead: another nineteen years of development to get you through childhood and a lifetime beyond, still waiting.

A radical rebirth

I think it is the same with being 'born again' into God's kingdom. I suspect this is rarely, if ever, an isolated event that just happens easily. I suspect it usually involves a certain amount of pain. Perhaps God does sometimes miraculously change people all of a sudden. In my experience, though, being 'born again' is usually a long process of nurture and development, maybe with a crisis point in the middle, but never the end of the story. I think for most people to find a meaningful relationship with God, others have invested in them, prayed for them, related to them, helped them to understand. Somehow, unseen, God is at work through all this, allowing their development in ways we can't understand.

Then there is the pain. For the person involved, choosing to follow Jesus is a step into the unknown. It will involve leaving the security of the world as he or she knows it, questioning values, and changing the way he or she functions.

Just as a baby's heart and circulation change dramatically at birth, Jesus seems to call us to a radical new way of living if we are to be in his kingdom. Reading the Sermon on the Mount and his other teaching in the gospels shows just how controversial this is – loving our enemies, putting others first, trusting God and not ourselves, rejecting violence, acknowledging our own vulnerability. I think when Jesus told Nicodemus that no one can see the kingdom of God without being born again, he was making one of the most fundamental statements of all time. 'Unless you are prepared to totally change the way you live in this world, you will not be part of my kingdom' was the kind of message he was trying to convey. This isn't some easy four-point prayer. It is a change as dramatic and painful as being born. I wonder how much we truly grasp this?

2

VULNERABILITY

*Can a mother forget the baby at her breast and have
no compassion on the child she has borne?*

- Isaiah 49:15

F ew things are as vulnerable as a newborn baby. When you were first born, my dearest Esther, you were dependent on your mother (and, to a lesser extent, on me). You were dependent on us for your food, for staying warm and clean, for sleeping safely. In the first few days, you spent most of your time sleeping, feeding, or being changed.

There are a few things that a baby needs to survive, which we can think of in terms of three basic requirements: nutrition, hygiene, and safety. I illustrate these in the diagram below.

A child's basic needs

Nutrition

Nutrition is the most basic, without which the baby will not have energy to stay warm, to grow and develop, or to fight off infections. But it is not just calories the baby needs. She needs the right amount of fluid to stay adequately hydrated; the right mix of carbohydrates, protein and fats to provide the energy and the building blocks for growth; roughage to keep her bowels functioning; vitamins and minerals as the essential micronutrients for the bones, organs, nervous system, and endocrine system to flourish; and antibodies to fight off infection.

One of the most amazing things about humans, as indeed with all mammals, is that the mother's milk provides all this and more, and seems to be perfectly regulated to the baby's needs. This is so finely attuned that the mother's milk alters over time, and even within an individual feed. While adults tend to regulate the times of feeds to suit their own schedules, if left to themselves, babies and mothers will usually regulate feeds in such a way that babies get just the right amount to thrive on. It is a telling fact that, in spite of years of research and millions of dollars of investment, baby-milk manufacturers have not been able to develop anything quite as perfect, individualised, and suited to a baby's needs as her mother's milk.

Skills for survival

Now I said that when you were born, you were totally dependent and vulnerable. That is not strictly true. Right from the moment you were born, you played an equal role in ensuring that you received the care you needed. You had a number of important skills which contributed to this partnership.

First, you could cry – and you made full use of this. That was one of the key signals that you were hungry and needed feeding. We learned quickly to respond to that. If you were hungry and crying, nothing stopped it better than being on your mother's breast. But you also cried when you were dirty and needed changing, or too cold, or too hot, or when you were bored, or just because you wanted some affection. And the amazing thing was that you had different cries for different needs. We didn't always get it right, but your mum in particular seemed to have an idea of what the matter was just from the way you cried.

Second, you had what is called a rooting reflex. This is one of a number of primitive reflexes that babies have. As a paediatrician, I marvel at these reflexes, using them as tools to help understand the baby's development.

The most unusual reflex is the Moro reflex. To achieve this, I hold the baby in my arms, lying backwards, facing me. One hand supports the baby's head, the other her body. I coo gently to the baby, getting her nice and relaxed, secure in my comforting arms. Without warning, I drop my hand down a couple of inches, so her head drops back (taking care not to drop it too far!). At this, the baby will open her eyes wide, throw her arms out to the side, open her clenched hands, and quiver for a moment, before drawing her hands and arms back in to her chest and finally relaxing again.

The rooting reflex is somewhat less dramatic. To elicit this, I simply stroke the baby's cheek. As I do so, the baby turns her head to the side I am stroking. If I stroke the other cheek, she will turn to that side. The importance of this is that it helps the baby to find her mother's nipple so as to latch on and feed.

This is followed by the suck reflex, which is probably one of the strongest reflexes: place something (such as a clean finger) in the baby's mouth and she will suck. Hard. I often used to watch you sucking at your mother's breast, and believe me, Esther, you used to suck as though your life depended on it – as of course it did. Put you on the breast and you would suck and suck until you were full.

These reflexes are crucial to survival. Without them, the baby would starve. If she tried to 'turn the other cheek' in response to a stroke, she would never latch on to be able to feed. If she waited till she was old enough to think about sucking, she would never get there. Unless there is something physically wrong with the baby, she will turn to find a source of milk and will suck as soon as anything is in her mouth. (I'm still not entirely sure what the Moro reflex is 'for'. Perhaps it has something to do with ensuring the parents handle their newborn baby with care and respect, avoiding dangerous actions like dropping her head that might elicit such a dramatic startle).

These primitive reflexes show us that the baby is designed to survive. This survival is instinctive, natural, and there from the moment of birth.

Hygiene

The next basic requirement, hygiene, is perhaps a bit more one-sided. When a baby is born, she is all wet and slimy and covered in a thick, creamy substance called *vernix*. This is probably important for protecting the baby's skin in utero, and as a barrier to infection, but if left, it would soon become a site of infection itself. So, straight after you were born, we rubbed you down with a towel (this also helped to get you dry and warm, of which more later).

Fairly soon after that, we gave you a bath. The first few baths were a bit of a shock for you, but you soon grew to love them. I remember you, my lovely daughter, enjoying the wonderful warm water and baby soap, the soft massages as we washed you down. And all this was a learning experience for the two of us as your parents.

As well as feeding and crying, the other thing babies are good at is excreting. What goes in has to come out. So you would wee and poo. And we would have to clean you up afterwards. If we failed to do so, your normal bodily functions would soon become a source of infection and harm. So we kept you fed, and we kept you clean.

Safety

Thirdly, we kept you safe. Being so small and vulnerable, there were lots of threats to you from the big, hostile environment that is the world.

Perhaps the greatest threat was the cold. England is not a warm country, but even in tropical climes, one of the greatest threats to newborn babies is hypothermia. Your physics will come in useful here – being a lot smaller than an adult, a baby has a greater surface area to volume ratio, and so will lose heat rapidly, particularly through the head. During the moments after birth, this is exacerbated further by the fact that she is wet. Hence the importance of a vigorous rub-down with a towel.

In my years as a hospital paediatrician, I used to enjoy supervising new paediatric trainees attending deliveries. Often, they would pussyfoot about, dabbing the new baby with a towel, worrying about whether she was breathing or not, and seemingly afraid of hurting the baby if they handled her too roughly – as if anything they might do could possibly compete with what she had just experienced coming through her mother's birth canal. I would grab the towel and show them how to rub the baby down as though she were a wet, muddy dog just come in from the park.

If the baby was a bit slow starting to breathe, this vigorous rub-down would normally stimulate her into taking a deep breath and crying her lungs out, thus avoiding the need to use oxygen or ventilation. In first aid and in basic life support, you are taught the ABC of airway, breathing, and circulation. The first thing a new paediatric trainee needs to do is to unlearn this for neonatal resuscitation, and instead start with DABC – dry, airway, breathing, circulation.

Thereafter, things were easier, but you still needed to be kept warm. So we would wrap you up carefully whenever we went out, with hat, coat, and mittens to protect those vulnerable parts. Then, of course, it all had to come off again when you came inside, since the risks of overheating are equally threatening. Indeed, that seems to be a key factor in at least some cases of sudden infant death syndrome – that some babies seem unable to regulate their temperatures properly, so if they are overwrapped, or in a particularly warm environment, they are at risk.

There were other threats too, in addition to temperature. There was the risk of infections, picked up from us, from other people, or just from the environment. Hence the importance of keeping you clean, but also of protecting you with good nutrition and with immunisations, and of responding if you seemed to be unwell.

In all of this, you probably did far more than we did, with your body's natural defence mechanisms preventing potential infections getting into your system in the first place, and antibodies fighting off any organisms that did get through. To start with, antibodies from your mum were circulating throughout your body and able to fight off most infections. Over the first weeks and months, these gradually worked their way out of your system, and were replaced by your own antibodies. So, once again, your body was perfectly designed to contribute to the all-important processes of survival.

Then, finally, there were risks of injury. To start with, you had no means of protecting yourself from injury, but neither did you have the means to get yourself into danger. In the early weeks, any risks of injury were small, but the responsibility rested with your mother and me to ensure you were safe. We would always be careful how we handled you or put you down, particularly watching out for your head, which, being large enough to accommodate your brain, was also heavy. At that early stage, your neck muscles were not strong enough to protect it, so we needed to support it carefully.

One of the amazing things about a child's development is that it is all so perfectly matched. As you gained the strength and ability to lift your head and move about more, so your muscle strength was matched to protect your head and body. And, even more impressively, you started to develop new reflexes – the protective reflexes. But more on those later.

God, the nursing mother

Reflecting on this vulnerability and a baby's basic needs, I think there is a lot we can learn about being 'born again' and becoming like a little child.

If I have understood Jesus correctly, we need to recognise our dependency – on him and on others – in order to see his kingdom. Like newborn babies, we need feeding.

It is interesting that the Bible explores this concept quite widely – from God providing Adam and Eve with good food in the garden, Yahweh's provision of manna for the Israelites in the desert, various indications in the Psalms and Prophets of God feeding his people, right through to Jesus feeding the multitudes and, indeed, being tempted himself by food in the wilderness. It seems as though God used food to emphasise people's dependence on his providence. And for those who do depend on him, God will be faithful.

In the context of feeding, we can also enter into a whole new understanding of God's nature. Far too much of our 'Christian' understanding of God is bounded by masculine pronouns and images: Father, Lord, Master, King. And yet the Bible, creation, and our own experience suggest that the almighty Holy One is far greater than any limitations our culture and language might impose. If God created humankind in the divine image – male and female – then God is surely both male and female, encompassing all that is good in both masculine and feminine.

In a wonderful verse in Isaiah, the prophet uses the illustration of a nursing mother: 'Can a mother forget the baby at her breast and have no compassion on the child she has borne?' Impossible as that may seem, Isaiah contrasts that with God's steadfast love: 'Though she may forget, I will not forget you! See, I have engraved you on the palms of my hands; your walls are ever before me.'[12]

This image of God as a nursing mother is so, so powerful. It cuts through all our stereotypes of a vengeful, stern judge or an omnipotent, unapproachable creator. Instead we see a different side of God's character – tender, passionate, caring, vulnerable. It invites us to come to God in such a different way. We come, not so much as miserable sinners cowering beneath 'his' judgement and in need of repentance and atonement, but as beloved children invited to nestle into 'her' bosom, to be cradled in her arms, to be enfolded in her love. A nursing mother does not place demands on her baby; she takes her up in her arms to love her and cherish her.

---

[12] Isaiah 49:15,16.

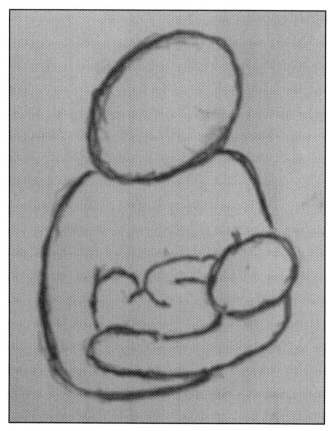

Can a mother forget the baby at her breast?

This is challenging; it challenges our preconceptions of who God is and what God is like. It also challenges our approach to the Holy One. Can we come to God as vulnerable, newborn babies, willing to put aside our pride and be accepted into her loving embrace? If we can, this move to become like a little child carries with it a wonderful promise of God's tender, embracing, steadfast love for us.

Becoming dependent

In the context of the kingdom of God, our nutritional needs are not simply the physical needs we have already explored. Jesus himself highlighted this, referring back to the manna in the desert and quoting Deuteronomy: 'He humbled you, causing you to hunger and then feeding you with manna, which neither you nor your fathers had known, to teach you that man does not live on bread alone but on every word that comes from the mouth of the Lord.'[13]

The parallels here are really striking. If we are to be born again in God's kingdom, we need to allow God to humble us and make us dependent. This is a dependency on God's Word. In order to survive and grow, we need to be feeding on God's Word in all its manifestations – in Scripture, nature, relationships, the traditions of the Church, our own inner nudgings. We need to regularly take it in, lingering over it and coming back to it again and again. The apostle Peter urges his readers, 'Like newborn babies, crave pure spiritual milk, so that by it you may grow up in your salvation.'[14]

This is a call to drink long and deep, to take time to contemplate and reflect, to be still. When you were a baby, I used to love watching you, my precious daughter, feeding at your mother's breast. So often you would be desperate to latch on and start sucking. You would race away, yearning to get that milk into you. Then gradually you would become more and more still, pausing occasionally just to look into your mother's eyes as she looked into yours, a beautiful bond of love between you. And finally, as your stomach was full, you would simply rest in her arms, content and satisfied, while deep within you your body started its wonderful work of digestion, transforming that milk into the life-giving energy and nutrients you needed.

---

13   Deuteronomy 8:3.
14   1 Peter 2:2.

Weaning

As you grew from a tiny infant, you gradually moved on from your mother's milk. We weaned you, introducing solid foods, till eventually you were no longer dependent on your mother as the source of your nutrition. So, as we grow in our spiritual lives, we need to progress from 'pure milk' to 'solid food': 'Anyone who lives on milk, being still an infant, is not acquainted with the teaching about righteousness. But solid food is for the mature, who by constant use have trained themselves to distinguish good from evil.'[15] So we need to move on, to grow and develop, and to progress from just reading God's Word to exploring it, understanding it, and applying it in our lives.

It has been such a joy to me as your father to watch you grow over these years. First as a child, then as a young person, you discovered your own spiritual journey, learning to engage with God's revelation in different ways, to question, explore, and apply it in your own life.

I too have been through my own journey of growth from dependency to maturity. But now, as I reflect on these words of Jesus, I wonder whether they are a call to us not to lose that initial dependency on pure, spiritual milk. Over these past years, I have found myself more and more drawn to a life of quiet contemplation. I yearn to rest in God's arms, to go deeper into the mystery of the Holy, Loving One, to drink deeply of that nurturing, satisfying milk of love, peace, and joy, to know that I am God's beloved child.

Becoming like a little child means situating oneself in the place where we know we are God's beloved. Surely this is the key to entering God's kingdom. The author Henri Nouwen captures this well:

Becoming the Beloved is the origin and the fulfilment of the life of the Spirit. I say this because, as soon as we catch a glimpse of this truth, we are put on a journey in search of the fullness of that truth and we will not rest until we can rest in that truth. From the

---

[15]   Hebrews 5:13-14.

moment we claim the truth of being the Beloved, we are faced with the call to become who we are. Becoming the Beloved is the great spiritual journey we have to make.[16]

Cleansing

Second, as children in God's kingdom, we need attention to hygiene. Young babies are quite remarkable in their capacity to fill their nappies. Stuff goes in one end, and stuff comes out the other. And what comes out needs to be cleaned away – regularly. Just as a newborn baby needs to be cleaned, so we need to be cleaned of all the dirt and filth that accumulates in us. This cannot just be a one-off cleaning, but needs to be regular and ongoing.

The whole symbolism of baptism is really important here. In the gospels, the people came to John by the Jordan. He baptised them as they confessed their sins and were made clean and ready for the kingdom of God, which, as he pointed out, was near.[17] So we, if we are going to be part of God's kingdom, need to confess our sins and be washed clean. Your baptism, dear Esther, was more than just a sign of commitment for you. It was a sacrament demonstrating God's forgiveness, cleansing, and restoration of you to be who he made you to be.

I think we tend to lose this a bit, particularly in some of our emphasis on Jesus as our loving friend. We must acknowledge that we are tainted and need to be made clean: 'Cleanse me with hyssop, and I shall be clean; wash me, and I shall be whiter than snow.'[18] The Anglican and other established liturgies, with their regular confession and absolution, capture this really well. I think we need

---

[16]   H. Nouwen. *Life of the beloved.* New York: Crossroad Publishing, 2007.

[17]   Matthew 3:1–12.

[18]   Psalm 51:7.

to rediscover how to build this into a daily routine of acknowledging our need before God and coming to him in humility and repentance. Then there is the dirt that accumulates from outside, as well as that within. By virtue of our involvement in the world, we will be tainted by it. We will inevitably be affected and influenced by the subtle messages of advertising and the media, the values of our friends, and the things we hear, read, and see. This is not to say that we should try and withdraw, Amish-like, from the world. A baby whose parents tried to keep her from ever getting dirty would not thrive and develop. She could potentially be in danger through not having been exposed to antigens in a way that allowed her to build up antibodies to fight off more threatening exposures. So we need to get into the world and to get our hands dirty. We then need to acknowledge this and once again allow God to cleanse us.

This repentance and cleansing is a prerequisite to engaging more fruitfully with the world around us. We are soiled by our own sin, the things we struggle with, the hurts and wounds we have experienced. Oh, how we need to accept all that, recognise and confess our struggles, and allow God to cleanse and heal us: 'If we don't really know how to attend to the reality that is our own inner turmoil, we shall fail in responding to the needs of someone else.'[19]

I notice this a lot in my work as a paediatrician with abused children and with grieving families – there is a lot of mess in the world, and it hurts. Sometimes I have come away from a medical examination, having heard about and seen the abuse that a parent has inflicted on his or her child, and I feel dirty, contaminated. Watching a film or hearing on the news about some dreadful atrocity committed elsewhere, I feel some of the guilt of association. I am part of fallen humanity, a humanity that sins, that suffers, and that needs God's redemption. I think, in some mysterious way, our tears are part of this cleansing act of God. When we cry, whether over our own pain, brokenness, and sin, or over the sin and suffering which

---

[19]   R. Williams. *Silence and honey cakes*. Oxford: Lion Hudson, 2003, 26.

we encounter in the world around us, our tears themselves bring cleansing and healing.

Protection

Finally there is our need for safety. The world is a dangerous place. If we are to live as part of God's kingdom, we need to recognise our dependence on God for safety and protection. The Bible is full of allusions to God's protecting grace, again with both feminine and masculine aspects.

> How often have I longed to gather your children together, as a hen gathers her chicks under her wings.[20]

> The name of the Lord is a strong tower, the righteous run to it and are safe.[21]

> The Lord is my strength and my shield; my heart trusts in him, and I am helped.[22]

Like infants, we are vulnerable and need protection. The dangers we face may be heightened when we choose to follow Jesus. If we become like little children, we make ourselves vulnerable. Perhaps that is why the Psalms are so full of references to the psalmists' enemies, and why Peter talks about the devil prowling around 'like a roaring lion looking for someone to devour.'[23] I wonder whether we may have lost sight of some of this, tending to assume that we

---

[20]   Luke 13:34.
[21]   Proverbs 18:10.
[22]   Psalm 28:7.
[23]   1 Peter 5:8.

are strong and secure, rather than acknowledging that each of us, if we are seeking to follow Jesus, is vulnerable and could easily be led astray or simply drift away from him.

I think the advice of St Paul, to 'put on the whole armour of God so that you can take your stand against the devil's schemes',[24] is really helpful here – reminding ourselves of our salvation, using the truth of God's Word, clothing ourselves with righteousness, stepping out with the gospel, holding on to our faith, and using the gifts of God's Spirit and the Word of God as weapons to help us live for God.

The humble God

Becoming like a little child takes humility. It requires us to make ourselves vulnerable. This is not something we find easy. One of the most staggering aspects of the Gospel, though, is that by taking this step of humility, we are actually following in God's footsteps.

One of my favourite parts of E.B. White's book *Charlotte's Web* is when the spider Charlotte writes different words in her web describing Wilbur the pig: 'TERRIFIC, RADIANT, SOME PIG'. Eventually, at a loss for superlatives to describe him, she writes one final word: 'HUMBLE'.[25] This is not a word we typically associate with celebrity or greatness. Certainly it is not a word humans would normally associate with God. At least, not until Jesus came along: tiny, vulnerable, wrapped in cloths, and lying in a manger.

God: immortal, invisible, and the great I Am; Creator of the rolling spheres; the One whose hands flung stars into space, who spoke and the world came into being, who breathed life into all living creatures; omnipotent, omniscient, omnipresent; thrice holy; the majestic Ruler of creation, from whom the angels themselves hide their faces, and before whom every knee will one day bow.

---

[24]   Ephesians 6:11.
[25]   E.B. White. *Charlotte's web*. London: Puffin, 2003, 106, 129.

This God became a baby, vulnerable and dependent. Perhaps that is the most shocking aspect of the Christian gospel. How could the almighty God possibly submit to being wrapped in cloths and laid in a manger, to having to cry for food, to having his bottom wiped by a young girl? The whole concept flies in the face of rational human thought.

It is shocking. But it is also wonderful and mysterious. Paul, who describes Jesus as 'the image of the invisible God',[26] in whom 'God was pleased to have all his fullness dwell',[27] also claims that Jesus, 'being in very nature God, did not consider equality with God something to be grasped, but made himself nothing, taking the very nature of a servant, being made in human likeness'.[28] He points out that Jesus 'humbled himself and became obedient to death – even death on a cross!'[29] So God, in Jesus, knows what it is to voluntarily humble himself. That he does this for us is amazing.

A call to humility

We find it very difficult to be humble. We always want other people to think the best of us. Often we exaggerate our own attributes or try to hide our weaknesses so we appear better than we truly are. We also like to think that we are resilient, that we can get by, and that things won't hurt us. So Jesus's call to 'be born again' and to 'become like a little child' is a call to humble ourselves. It is a truly radical call.

We have already explored a bit of what it means to be dependent. In calling us to take these steps, Jesus is calling us to acknowledge our vulnerability, to accept that we are not as strong as we think we are, and even to make ourselves more dependent on others. It is perhaps the hardest call upon those who truly want to follow Jesus.

---

[26] Colossians 1:15.
[27] Colossians 1:19.
[28] Philippians 2:6–7.
[29] Philippians 2:8.

Jesus himself likens it to carrying a cross: 'If anyone would come after me, he must deny himself and take up his cross daily and follow me.'[30] Paul, too, exhorts us that our 'attitude should be the same as Christ Jesus' in becoming humble.[31]

It seems to me that, throughout the Bible, humility is one of the characteristics that God most loves to see in us.

> This is the one I esteem: he who is humble and contrite in spirit.[32]

> He crowns the humble with salvation.[33]

In his classic prayer of repentance, David points out that God does not delight in sacrifice or burnt offerings, but that 'the sacrifices of God are a broken spirit; a broken and contrite heart, O God, you will not despise.'[34] And the prophet Micah highlights three things that God requires of us: 'to act justly, and to love mercy, and to walk humbly with your God.'[35] I suspect it is the last of those that we find most difficult. We can accept the need for justice and mercy, but humility is a different matter.

And yet, as we see in Jesus's nativity, God's call to humility is not a vain request that is impossible to fulfil. By taking on himself the humility of the incarnation, God has shown us that it can be done. Our humble God has called us to a truly radical humility that goes beyond the somewhat false humility of many traditional prayers and sacrifices. It is a humility that truly acknowledges that we can't make it on our own, that we need help – a lot of help. It is

---

30   Luke 9:23.
31   Philippians 2:5.
32   Isaiah 66:2.
33   Psalm 149:4.
34   Psalm 51:17.
35   Micah 6:8.

a humility that will identify with those who are vulnerable – with the poor, the outcast, the oppressed.

That, perhaps, is one of the key reasons why humility is so important. It is only through humility that we can possibly include all in God's kingdom. Those who are broken, vulnerable, and cast out of society are so often stuck. They do not have the resources to raise themselves out of their brokenness, any more than a baby has the resources to raise herself from her infancy.

Complaining

There is one final aspect of being born again and becoming like a little child that perhaps isn't so obvious in what Jesus was saying, but which I think is probably really important. When things go wrong, babies complain. We tend to assume that, as Christians, we shouldn't really complain, that it is wrong to grumble, and that we should just 'grin and bear it'.

But the Bible doesn't anywhere tell us to grin and bear it. If anything, quite the opposite. The Psalms, in particular, are full of complaint. Israel seems to be positively encouraged, if things aren't going her way, to complain about it. As adults we tend to become very adept at hiding our feelings; if we are upset or angry, we tend to bottle it up inside rather than let it out. Perhaps, in telling us to become like little children, Jesus was also encouraging us to learn again to express our feelings.

As a baby, if you decided you were hungry and hadn't been fed, or if you woke up and your mum wasn't there, you would let her know about it in no uncertain terms. You considered it your right to be fed, cared for, and comforted, and we jolly well ought to know that.

So perhaps with God, when things aren't going well or we feel God has been unjust, uncaring, or simply silent, we too should let our loving, heavenly parent know about it rather than bottling it up and becoming cynical.

The psalmist certainly doesn't shy away from expressing his feelings to God:

> O my God, I cry out by day, but you do not answer,
> by night, and am not silent.[36]

> Why do you stand far off, O God, so mute, hiding
> yourself from your people in time of our need?[37]

> How long, O Lord? Will you forget me forever?
> How long will you hide your face from me? How
> long must I wrestle with my thoughts and every day
> have sorrow in my heart?[38]

I don't know why God so often seems to be silent and oblivious to our suffering. But, like a little child, I don't want to just accept that passively. Rather, when God does seem to be silent or uncaring, I want to let him know about it.

---

[36]   Psalm 22:2.
[37]   Psalm 10, *Psalms for a pilgrim people*, 18.
[38]   Psalm 13:1–2.

3

LOVE

*I have loved you with an everlasting love; I
have drawn you with loving-kindness*

- Jeremiah 31:3

Nutrition, hygiene, and safety are not all that a baby needs to survive. There is an overarching, even more fundamental element without which a child will not thrive: love. We can add this, therefore, to our diagram of a child's basic needs.

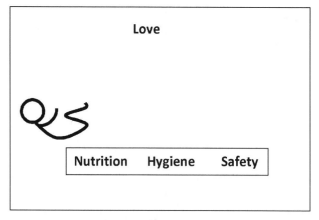

A child's basic needs (II)

The effect of an absence of love is seen most devastatingly in children raised in institutions. Researchers in the middle of the last century observed children who had grown up in orphanages. Many of these children, in spite of adequate nutrition, hygiene, and safety, just did not thrive. Failure to respond to emotional needs, a lack of stimulation, or even the absence of a consistent person to relate to can all lead to negative outcomes for children in institutions.[39]

Such emotional deprivation can lead to developmental delays, difficulties in socialisation, and emotional and behavioural problems in later childhood and adult life. It can also result in adverse physical effects, including poor growth. The relationship between institutional care, lack of emotional input, and outcomes is not straightforward, though. Many children do well in spite of the damaging effects of such care. Some of the long-term outcomes of institutionalization can be ameliorated by early stimulation and consistent care. Conversely, many children growing up within their own families will not receive the parental love they need to grow. Nevertheless, the fact remains that the absence of a loving parent in the first years of life can have devastating long-term effects on a child.

Institutional care

As I think about the impact of institutional care on children, two contrasting experiences stand out for me from my own childhood in Hong Kong. The first, my dear Esther, is from the orphanage where we adopted my sister and your aunt, Mei Ling.

---

[39]   The research in this area has been well summarised by the psychologist Michael Rutter. See M. Rutter. 'Maternal deprivation, 1972–1978: new findings, new concepts, new approaches'. *Child development*, 1979; 50: 283–305

We don't know a lot about Mei Ling's early background. We know she was born with a cleft lip and palate and was probably abandoned by her mother because of that. She spent her first three years in an orphanage. Her cleft lip and palate were repaired, she was fed and physically cared for, but she almost certainly did not receive any love, emotional care, or stimulation during those critical early years.

Although I was very young at the time, I vaguely remember visiting her in the orphanage. My impression was of lots of babies and toddlers, all sitting in their cots, clean and well fed, but with no toys and no one picking them up to cuddle them. I seem to remember many of them crying.

That was such a contrast to the Home of Loving Faithfulness (HOLF), another orphanage which I had the privilege to visit several times as I was growing up. The children at HOLF were all disabled, mostly with severe learning difficulties; many had physical impairments as well. These children needed constant physical care. But what was so striking about HOLF was the overwhelming love in the place. The orphanage was run by two old ladies, Wendy and Valerie, and they and the younger volunteers who helped them seemed to love those children as though they were their own. The children were given loads of hugs; they were sung to, cuddled, played with, and held. Whenever any one of them cried, someone would go and gently hold the child, staying there until the distress abated. What I saw in those children's eyes, in spite of their difficulties, was life. They were loved and valued, and they knew it.

While I was too young to recognise it then, I have seen many children since whose eyes convey something very different. It is a look we refer to as 'frozen watchfulness'. Children who have been emotionally abused or neglected typically show this. They may attentively watch everything that is going on around them. They don't miss a thing. And yet they don't interact. It worries me when I see children like that. Most young children, when they come to see me in my clinics, relax, play, smile, and laugh. Some get distressed and cry. That doesn't worry me. But the ones who neither laugh nor cry concern me. In these children's eyes, I don't see life and love. I just see emptiness.

I suspect my sister Mei Ling was like that when we adopted her. I remember the journey home after we collected her from the orphanage. She cried all the way. As a 5-year-old who had only ever known a loving family, and full of the excitement of acquiring a new sister, I couldn't understand why she was crying. Why wasn't she excited and full of joy now that she knew she was becoming part of our family? At that age I couldn't possibly understand the trauma of separating from all you have ever known, even if that known environment was far from loving.

Still, all that changed as Mei Ling grew up as part of our family. She learned to smile, to laugh, to have fun. She learned to read and write, to play, to draw, to make things, and to do all that other children do. She went to school, had friends, performed in school plays, and sat exams. She grew tall and attractive, with a lovely, winsome smile.

I'm not sure I was the best brother she could have hoped for, but perhaps I wasn't that different from other brothers – always walking several steps in front of her on my way to school, excluding her from some of my games, teasing her or winding her up when it suited me. At other times, though, we would play together. I think, for all our faults, we weren't a bad family. The one thing that was never in doubt was that we loved her. Your Granny, Granddad, Auntie, and I all loved her. She was a part of our family, and that would never change.

But, while Mei Ling grew and developed, something was always missing. All along she struggled with relating to other people. She found it very difficult to trust others. Above all, I think she could never quite believe that other people loved her.

Auntie Mei Ling died when you were just ten. We were all devastated by her death. At her funeral I was really moved to see how many of her work colleagues came along, and how much they too seemed to have been affected by her death. She was loved and valued even by people who had only known her through her work. But I suspect that the impact of those first three years without love had gone far deeper than any of us really appreciated, and Auntie Mei Ling never fully knew just how much she was loved.

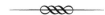

Affection and expectation

Love is vital to a child's development and sense of well-being. But what is it about love, and specifically a parent's love, that is so important? What form does a parent's love take? Why is it so crucial to a child's development? And what does this have to tell us about being born again and becoming like a little child?

I want to be fairly generic here, and not to distinguish between a father's love and a mother's love. Although I believe there are some differences, there are probably more similarities, and both are important. As you were growing, dear Esther, your mother and I both loved you intensely. The way we loved you and the way we expressed that love was perhaps very different. I suspect, though, that those differences reflected more of our individual personalities than any inherent differences in our gender or relationship to you.

I have thought a lot about parenting, both in terms of how we have brought you and your brother Joseph up, and in broader terms as it impacts on my work with cared for and abused children, and with caring and abusive parents. I think there is a lot we can learn about God's relationship to us from looking at parenting. Similarly, there is a lot we can learn about parenting through considering God's nature as a parent.

Some of the most helpful research on parenting has described it in terms of two core dimensions: 'responsiveness' and 'demandingness'.[40] From these, four basic types of parenting can be drawn: neglectful, indulgent, authoritarian, and authoritative.[41] I prefer to characterise the two core dimensions as 'affection' and 'expectation'. These dimensions are illustrated in the following diagram:

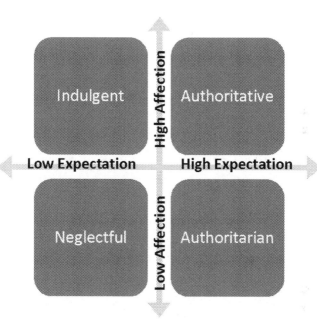

Dimensions of parenting

Dimensions of parenting

The dimension of affection perhaps aligns most closely to the roles typically attributed to a mother: tenderness, response to her

---

[40] D. Baumrind. 'Current patterns of parental authority'. *Developmental psychology monograph*, 1971; 4 (1 part 2).

[41] E. Macoby and J. Martin. 'Socialization in the context of the family: parent-child interaction'. *Handbook of child psychology.* Ed. P. Mussen. New York: Wiley, 1983.

child's needs, provision, spending time with her child, and so on. In contrast, the dimension of expectation is typically associated with fathers and includes stimulation, provision of opportunities, the setting of boundaries, and discipline of his child. I believe both are crucially important to healthy development.

It is easy to see how neglectful parenting is harmful to children. This may be accompanied by physical neglect – parents failing to provide for the basic physical needs of food, shelter, clothing, or hygiene. However, even where these are provided, emotional neglect can occur if a parent does not provide her child with affection, or if a child lacks stimulation, discipline, and boundaries. The extremes of this are what we see in some children reared in uncaring institutions. But we also see it to lesser degrees in many ordinary families.

Such emotional abuse can have long-term impacts on the child's development. The lack of affection may leave the child feeling unloved and unvalued; a lack of stimulation will slow her development; a lack of supervision, boundaries, and discipline will put her at risk of accidents and injuries or of self-harmful behaviour.

A child who grows up in a home that ranks high in affection but low in expectation experiences indulgent parenting. Such children may become spoilt. They may appreciate the affection they are shown, they may have all that they could want or need, but in fact they do not truly feel loved. How often have you heard parents say, whether in books, films, or real life, 'I don't understand where we have gone wrong; we've given her everything, and still she has turned against us'?

Without expectation, a child will not learn how to strive, to hope, and to achieve. Nor will she learn to look beyond herself to the needs of others, or learn how to discipline herself. While indulgent parenting may not immediately seem harmful, in effect it is not giving a child the love she truly needs.

The opposite pole, with high expectation but low affection, is the typical authoritarian home. Parents may have huge expectations of their child, they may impose strict discipline, or they may drive their child to achieve. But this is not balanced by the loving attention the child needs. A child growing up in such a home may herself be driven and may feel the need always to prove herself, considering herself never to be good enough.

Sadly, this type of parenting is, or at least has been, relatively common among churchgoers, and may be accompanied by excessively harsh discipline. This may stem from an overemphasis on sin in a child's life, and from too much reliance on a few biblical references to corporal punishment.

The concept that we are all sinful and, as such, separated from God, is encapsulated in Paul's letter to the Romans: 'For all have sinned and fall short of the glory of God.'[42] It is hinted at in David's psalm of repentance: 'Surely I was sinful at birth, sinful from the time my mother conceived me.'[43] However, in both those settings and elsewhere where Paul refers to our sinful nature, this sinfulness is linked to the possibility of redemption.[44]

While these passages emphasise that we are all affected by sin and cut off from God, and while we can see the effects of that even from a very early stage, I think it is dangerous to extrapolate from that to assume that all children are inherently evil and need to have that evil driven out of them. As we shall explore later, the Bible places an equal, if not greater, emphasis on humankind being inherently good and loved by God.

An overemphasis on sin has, I think, been one root of a strong message in some church circles regarding the use of physical punishment. This is seemingly condoned by four proverbs:

He who spares the rod hates his son.[45]

---

[42] Romans 3:23.
[43] Psalm 51:5.
[44] Romans 5:12–21; 1 Corinthians 15:20–22.
[45] Proverbs 13:24.

Folly is bound up in the heart of a child, but the rod of discipline will drive it far from him.[46]

Do not withhold discipline from a child; if you punish him with the rod, he will not die. Punish him with the rod and save his soul from death.[47]

The rod of correction imparts wisdom.[48]

I was brought up with physical punishment as a part of discipline, and indeed, when you were younger, I used physical punishment with both you and your brother. I am, however, rethinking this, and I am no longer convinced that it is the best way of disciplining a child.

It is potentially very dangerous to form a strong doctrine and praxis on the basis of a few verses which may have significant cultural overtones. The principle of discipline is crucially important, as we shall see below, but that does not necessarily mean that it has to rely on physical punishment.

Certainly where it is taken to extremes, physical punishment can be horrendously abusive. In my work I have come across children who have been physically harmed and even killed as a result of physical punishment. While not all would consider physical punishment per se to be abusive, it very clearly can result in severe abuse. It seems to me now that it is far better to avoid that risk and rely instead on more positive, non-physical approaches to discipline.

Where expectations and discipline are high and are not balanced by the restraining hand of affection, the child is at risk of harm.

---

[46]   Proverbs 22:15.
[47]   Proverbs 23:13–14.
[48]   Proverbs 29:15.

Authoritative parenting

This brings us to the fourth parenting style: authoritative parenting. As you have probably worked out, my precious daughter, this is what your mum and I have striven to achieve in bringing up you and your brother. In this style of parenting, both affection and expectation are high. The child is loved and valued and receives a lot of affection from her parents. She is cuddled and affirmed, comforted when upset, and celebrated just for being who she is.

One aspect of authoritative parenting is that it takes time. There has been a vogue in Western society for emphasising the importance of parents spending 'quality time' with their children. This has sometimes been used to excuse the fact that many parents spend a small quantity of time with their children. These parents assert that if the time they spend with their children is packed and intense, that will make up for a lack of quantity.

The truth is that children need 'quantity time'. In a sense it almost doesn't matter what that time is filled with; children just need their parents to be there. We have been immensely privileged that your mum was able to work from home and so was around while you and Joe were growing up. I too, when you were younger, was able to spend some time working part-time, and so was around a lot more than I might otherwise have been. Many parents do not have that privilege but still manage to spend time with their children – perhaps even more so than we have.

I guess what is important here is setting priorities. If we, as parents, see our children as a priority, we will spend time with them.

The other dimension in authoritative parenting is that of high expectation – not excessive, as in unbalanced authoritarian parenting, but high. The authoritative parent sees the potential in his child and strives to enable her to reach that potential. That is why your mother and I may have seemed to nag you at times when you were growing up. This was because we loved you, and we wanted you to do your best – whether that was in your school work, in your hobbies, in your friendships, in relating to your family, or in your walk with God.

This kind of expectation takes the form of opportunities and stimulation, and also of discipline. When you were young, Esther, we read to you. We would play with you, talk with you, and encourage your development. Later on, we tried to provide you with opportunities of your own, to develop further and explore your own identity and passions. But we also set boundaries and tried to instil appropriate discipline.

Boundaries create safety and security. They are essential when a child is young and unable to appreciate dangers or protect herself from harm. As she grows, the boundaries may be relaxed, allowing her to explore and venture out more. The aim in this is to enable her to develop her own self-discipline.

Although I have expressed caution over the use of physical punishment, the principle of discipline is, I think, extremely important and rooted in a biblical understanding of parenting. It pervades the book of Proverbs, and indeed comes up time and time again throughout the Bible:

> Train a child in the way he should go, and when he is old he will not turn from it.[49]

> These commandments that I give you today are to be upon your hearts. Impress them on your children. Talk about them when you sit at home and when you walk along the road, when you lie down and when you get up.[50]

It is interesting that throughout the book of Proverbs, the references to discipline are mostly linked to blessing and life:

---

[49] Proverbs 22:6.
[50] Deuteronomy 6:6–7.

Discipline your son, for in that there is hope.[51]

The corrections of discipline are the way to life.[52]

Authoritative parenting combines high affection with high expectation. It is that style of parenting that brings life, health, and development for a child. These two qualities of authoritative parenting are components of the love that is so essential to a child's development. We can add these to our model of a child's needs.

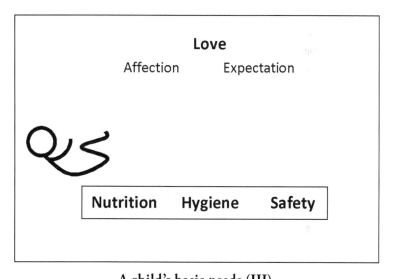

A child's basic needs (III)

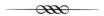

God, the Good Parent

It seems to me that Jesus's exhortation to 'become like a little child' is as much an invitation as a challenge. It is an invitation to enter into a relationship with God as our loving parent: the One who

---

51   Proverbs 19:18.
52   Proverbs 6:23.

encapsulates all that it means to be a good parent – both father and mother. God, who created us, loves each one of us unconditionally. The Holy One sees each of us as we are intended to be, created in his image. Our creator is full of expectation and hope that we can become that complete person. God, El Shaddai, the one who nurtures and sustains us, longs to enfold us in his arms, hold us secure, and love us.

Jesus seems to take much further the Old Testament concept of God as Father, addressing God as 'Abba, Father'[53] and instructing his disciples to pray 'our Father in heaven'.[54] Indeed, Jesus hardly ever addresses or refers to God as anything other than 'Father'. In telling us that we need to be born again, Jesus is inviting us to come into a wonderful, loving relationship with his perfect Father.

My dearest Esther, while I love you so much, God's kind of love is much greater than anything you have experienced from me. While I may aspire to be an authoritative parent, loving and kind, combining affection and expectation, I fail. God, however, does not fail. If we look at God as Jesus portrayed him, we can see what fatherhood is truly meant to be like.

One of the most striking things that I notice in how God's fatherhood is portrayed is that, just as in the models presented above, he combines expectation with affection. But God's affection always comes first and far exceeds any element of expectation.

We see this first in God's relationship to Adam. When God created the heavens and the earth, he looked on it and saw that it was good. And at the pinnacle of the Genesis account of creation, we read:

> God created man in his own image;
> in the image of God he created him;
> male and female he created them.[55]

---

[53] Mark 14:36.

[54] Matthew 6:9.

[55] Genesis 1:27.

God goes on to bless them. He provides for them. When he saw all that he had made, he saw that 'it was very good'.[56] So right at the heart of the creation story, we see God's love expressed in affection, pride, blessing, and provision.

Alongside that affection and blessing, we also see God putting in place expectations. On the one hand, he does so in terms of a challenge or commission. He tells Adam to be fruitful and multiply, to fill the earth and subdue it, and to rule over every living creature. He gives Adam the task of taking care of the garden of Eden.

On the other hand, God sets boundaries. 'You are free to eat from any tree in the garden; but you must not eat from the tree of the knowledge of good and evil, for when you eat of it you will surely die.'[57]

God set the boundaries in place for Adam's protection. When Adam ignored those boundaries, humankind suffered the consequences: the toil of working the ground, the labour of bearing children, the pain of broken relationships, and ultimately the taste of death.

But even in the curses of Genesis 2, we see God's gracious affection breaking through. He provides clothes for Adam and Eve, and again sets a boundary in place, to protect them from the even worse fate of living eternally with the consequences of their rebellion.

We see God's fatherhood also expressed in his relationship to Israel. Again he demonstrates a combination of affection and expectation, with affection prevailing. In calling Abraham, God sets him a challenge to leave his country and family, and gives him a commission to be a blessing to all people.[58] This too comes with God's promise of blessing: 'I will make you into a great nation and

---

[56]   Genesis 1:31.
[57]   Genesis 2:16–17.
[58]   Genesis 12:1–3.

I will bless you; I will make your name great, and you will be a blessing.'[59]

Throughout the Psalms and Prophets, we catch glimpses of God's fatherhood. One of the most inspiring examples of this is in Psalm 103:

> The Lord is compassionate and gracious,
> slow to anger, abounding in love.
> He will not always accuse,
> nor will he harbour his anger for ever …
> As a father has compassion on his children,
> so the Lord has compassion on those who fear him …
> from everlasting to everlasting
> the Lord's love is with those who fear him,
> and his righteousness with their children's children –
> with those who keep his covenant
> and remember to obey his precepts.[60]

In assuming the relationship of Father to us, God becomes vulnerable. Because, while fatherhood brings immense joy, it also brings pain, particularly when the love the father pours out on his child is not reciprocated. This anguish comes across poignantly in Hosea's prophecy:

> When Israel was a child, I loved him,
> and out of Egypt I called my son.
> But the more I called Israel,
> the further they went from me.
> They sacrificed to the Baals
> and they burned incense to images.

---

[59] Genesis 12:2.
[60] Psalm 103:8–18.

It was I who taught Ephraim to walk,
taking them by the arms;
but they did not realise it was I who healed them.
I led them with cords of human kindness,
with ties of love;
I lifted the yoke from their neck
and bent down to feed them.[61]

It is in that context that Jesus invites us to become like little children. We too have spurned God's fatherly love. We repeatedly rebel against God and fail to recognise his presence. But, like the prodigal son returning to his father, Jesus invites us to come back to God as our Father. Just as that father welcomed his son home, God will welcome us home into his loving embrace: 'While he was still a long way off, his father saw him and was filled with compassion for him; he ran to his son, threw his arms around him and kissed him.'[62]

---

61   Hosea 11:1–4.
62   Luke 15:20.

4

HUMANNESS

Jesus grew in wisdom and stature, and in favour with God and man.

- Luke 2:52

B abies do not remain as babies. One of the most inspiring aspects of my role as a paediatrician is watching the incredible process of transformation as small infants grow and develop into toddlers, children, and adolescents, and finally leave my care as mature adults. Likewise, it has been a privilege and joy to watch you, my daughter, gradually change from the small, vulnerable infant who came into the world all those years ago into the tall, beautiful, intelligent, and sociable young woman you are now, ready to leave home and make your own way in this world.

The only description we have of Jesus growing up is one small incident when he was 12 years old.[63] Jesus's family had been to Jerusalem to celebrate the Passover. On their way back to Nazareth with their relatives and friends, it took them a full day before they realised Jesus wasn't with them. Now, that might be considered negligent by today's standards, but was probably quite appropriate in

---

[63] Luke 2:41–52.

the context of first-century Jewish life. When they did not find him, his parents went back to Jerusalem and spent three days looking for him. Eventually they found him sitting in the temple courts, talking with the teachers there.

In a marvellous bit of understatement, Luke tells us that when they saw him, his parents were 'astonished'. His mother said to him, 'Son, why have you treated us like this? Your father and I have been anxiously searching for you.'[64] I can imagine that his mother said a lot more than that, and almost certainly in far less polite words. They obviously got over their misunderstanding though, and Jesus apparently returned to Nazareth and was obedient to them. Luke goes on to state that Jesus grew 'in wisdom and stature, and in favour with God and man.'[65]

Luke's description of Jesus's development suggests four domains or areas in which children grow and develop into adults: mental development ('wisdom'), physical development ('stature'), spiritual development ('favour with God') and social development ('favour with men'). We can add these, therefore, to our diagram, to demonstrate the process of child development. The development of these four areas takes place on the bedrock of satisfaction of a child's basic needs, and within the overarching context of unconditional parental love.

---

[64]   Luke 2:48.
[65]   Luke 2:52.

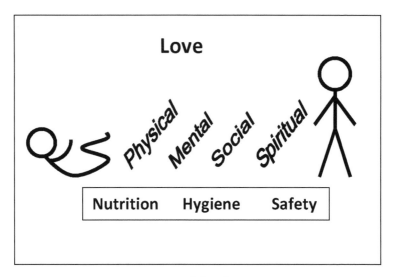

Domains of development

Human characteristics

These domains of development do not exist in isolation. It is all four that make us human. Take any one away and we would not be what we are. You can relate these four domains to the characteristics that distinguish us as human beings.

To start with the physical side of our development, two of the most distinguishing features of humans compared to other animals are our upright stance and our ability to use tools. On a mental level, we are cognizant beings, *Homo sapiens*. On a social level, we use language to communicate and have developed complex and far-reaching social structures and networks. And finally, we are spiritual beings. We are created to relate to God, to the world around us, to others, and to ourselves. These domains and their associated developmental tasks and characteristics are summarised in the following table.

Table: Human characteristics

Primary Domain	Developmental Tasks	Human Characteristic
Physical	Gross motor (locomotor and balance) Fine motor (eye-hand coordination)	Upright stance Use of tools
Mental	Naming Pattern recognition Memory Reason	Thinking Wisdom
Social	Hearing and language (comprehension) Speech and language (expression) Interactive social Self-care	Communication Social structures and networks Independence
Spiritual	Identity, emotions Empathy, justice, morals Wonder, discovery Searching, worship	Awareness of self Awareness of others Awareness of creation Awareness of God

With all our being

One of the most powerful aspects of Judaism and Christianity is that all these elements of our humanity are combined in our relationship to God. We are not just spiritual beings temporarily housed in physical bodies. We are human beings: physical, mental, social, and spiritual.

This is reflected in the great Shema prayer in Deuteronomy: '*Shema Yisrael Adonai eloheinu Adonai ehad*[66] ('Hear O Israel: the Lord our God, the Lord is one').[67] The prayer affirms the unity of God and his relationship to his people. It goes on to focus on our response to God: 'Love the Lord your God with all your heart and with all your soul and with all your strength.'[68] This response comes from the totality of our humanness.

Jesus himself reflected this, affirming this commandment as the greatest of all: 'Love the Lord your God with all your heart and with all your soul and with all your mind and with all your strength.'[69] These four domains in Mark's account seem to mirror the four domains we have considered above: we are to love the Lord our God with all our hearts (our social development, our relationships with others), with all our souls (our spiritual development, our emotions, the very core of who we are), with all our minds (our cognitive development, our thoughts and reason), and with all our strength (our physical development, our tangible human bodies).

While the precise words may differ between Matthew's and Mark's accounts[70] and the original Torah, the principle is the same: it's our whole humanness that counts. We worship God with the entirety of our being – body, mind, heart, and soul.

We do not try to escape the material world of our being, as some Eastern philosophies would have us do. Nor do we separate the material and the spiritual, as in much of the Greek thought that so dominates our modern, Western (and even much of our 'Christian') view of the world. Rather, we engage with ourselves, others, our world, and God in the nitty-gritty, everyday reality of our lives, with

---

[66]   S. Schoenberg. *Jewish prayers: the Shema.* Jewish Virtual Library. www.jewishvirtuallibrary.org/jsource/Judaism/shema.html Accessed 11.5.14.

[67]   Deuteronomy 6:4.

[68]   Deuteronomy 6:5.

[69]   Mark 12:30.

[70]   See Matthew 22:37 for the comparison.

all their gifts and limitations, their joys and their hurts, their order
and their messiness.

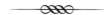

A new process of development

In asking us to become like little children, Jesus asks us to accept
our own vulnerability and to make ourselves dependent, on God and
on others. But he doesn't ask us to stay there. Rather, he is calling
us to a whole new process of development, one in which our hearts
and souls, and perhaps ultimately our bodies and minds too, will
become all that our Creator intended them to be.

Esther, my precious child, as I have observed you and other
children growing and developing, I have seen in that development
glimpses of how this deeper new development might take place.
Over the next four chapters, I would like to explore the different
domains of development, considering what it means to be human
and what distinguishes a mature adult from a baby.

I want to describe this in detail, as I think there are some
incredible lessons we can learn from children's development about
how we, as little children, can grow in God's kingdom. As I do
so, though, I want you to keep in mind that each of these is just a
convenient lens through which to see one facet of the totality of our
humanity. You will see through these chapters many ways in which
the domains overlap and are dependent on each other.

As you read these pages, my hope is that they will open up to
you a little more of what it means to be a human being, created in
God's image, and to worship God with all your heart and soul and
mind and strength.

5

STRENGTH

Physical Development

Those who hope in the Lord will renew their strength.
They will soar on wings like eagles; they will run and
not grow weary, they will walk and not be faint.

- Isaiah 40:31

Children grow. Their height, weight, and head circumference all increase. Most parents love to see how their children are growing – marking the years on their door frames, or recording the centiles on a growth chart.

The first year is a year of tremendous growth. By the time you were a year old, Esther, your length had increased by a half, your head circumference by a third, and your weight by more than two and a half times.

Thereafter things slow down a bit until puberty, when once again the child puts on a spurt of growth, along with further changes of sexual differentiation.

By the time you reached eighteen, dear Esther, you were about three and a half times taller than when you started. However, it seemed even more than that, as not only had you increased in length, but you had moved from lying supine to standing upright, and you had learned to move about. We have already seen that one of the distinctive features of humans is our upright stance. As you grew, you learned to sit, to roll from your back to your front, to lift up on your arms, and to tuck your knees under you to crawl. From there you learned to pull yourself up into a standing position, to cruise around the furniture, and eventually to launch out on your own two feet, independently walking.

Getting upright

It is fascinating to watch this take place. The whole process is finely tuned to enable the growing child to move and explore more as she gains in strength and in other abilities. A newborn baby, of course, is not completely inert, but wriggles and moves her limbs. Gradually she gains the skills to roll from side to side, then eventually to roll right over.

A young baby can be encouraged to develop the skill of rolling by holding an interesting toy in front of her. As she focuses on the toy, one gradually moves it to one side. She will follow it with her eyes, moving her head to the side as she does so. One then slowly moves it round towards the top of her head. The baby will try to follow it, moving her head, then her neck and shoulders, and then her trunk. Finally, as she gains the skill, she will twist her whole body over, spurred on by her inquisitiveness and her desire to follow the moving object.

On her front, a newborn baby will lie scrunched up, with her knees tucked under her, her arms tucked in to her side, and her head to one side. Gradually, from top to toe, her muscle strength increases, and she learns to lift up: first her head, then her shoulders, then her upper trunk on her arms. As she does so, her legs gradually straighten out from under her to lie flat along the floor. Then she starts to bring them back in again as she gets into a crawling position, lifting her whole body off the ground and preparing to move.

Meanwhile, she is also learning to get into a sitting position. At first, she can only do so when pulled up and supported by her parent. The young infant, placed in a sitting position, will flop forward, her head bent to the ground and her back a nice, smooth curve from her neck to her bottom. Gradually, again from top to bottom, she straightens up, first lifting her head, then her shoulders, and eventually sitting upright so she can look around at the world. As with her rolling, all this is motivated by a desire to see and explore the world around her.

From sitting and crawling, the infant then learns to stand. Initially with her parents' help, then on her own, she pulls herself up on anything to hand.

As she gains the strength and ability to sit upright, to crawl, and to stand, the young child also develops a remarkable set of protective reflexes, without which she would be even more vulnerable to the relentless forces of gravity. In sitting, she develops forward and sideways protective and righting reflexes – putting her hands out in front of her or to one side to protect herself if she loses her balance, then increasingly counteracting the forces of gravity to keep herself in a stable position with her centre of gravity above the base on which she is sitting.

At around nine to ten months, the infant develops a forward parachute reflex. This reflex will stay with her for the rest of her life and is one of the most powerful self-protective reflexes known. If you were to drop forward to the floor, without you having to think about it, your hands would go forward to protect yourself and break your fall. This reflex is so strong that it takes a huge effort of will to prevent it happening. In a very young infant, this reflex is not present. But it develops at just the right time, enabling the toddler to safely get upright and start walking.

Walking is one of the key aims of all this motor development. Once the toddler is upright, she can get around far more efficiently than through crawling or shuffling around on her bottom. This allows her to move around and explore her world, and at the same time to be upright, look around her, and see so much more.

This new-found freedom is a delight to the toddler and a nightmare for her parents. They can no longer leave her sitting safely with a pile of toys on the floor. Stair gates go up to protect her from steep falls. She is constantly watched as she moves about, and kept close when going out.

Using and losing

As well as allowing a child to move around effectively and to see and explore her world, an upright stance frees her hands to manipulate objects. This, together with that remarkable creation, the opposable thumb, enables an incredible range of fine motor talents – from building a tower of blocks, to using a pencil to draw and write, to creating intricate sculptures or performing beautiful musical compositions.

An intriguing developmental process takes place to support this development of manipulation. While, in her development of posture and mobility, we saw the infant acquire certain protective reflexes, in her fine motor development she has to lose certain inbuilt primitive reflexes that would otherwise hinder this development.

I'm not sure quite why we have these primitive reflexes, or what purpose they serve, but they are nevertheless there and remarkably strong. The most obvious of these is the palmar grasp reflex. If you place your finger across the palm of a newborn infant, the infant will immediately grasp your finger, and grasp it hard. It is sometimes possible to lift the baby's entire body weight simply by relying on the grasp reflex to stop her from falling.

This reflex, if it were to persist, would be frustratingly inconvenient. It would mean that every time you touched something with the palm of your hand or had something placed in your palm, you would immediately clench your fist. The baby needs to lose this reflex in order to learn to control her gripping, to direct it to hold those objects she wants to hold while releasing or leaving those she doesn't. As the grasp reflex weakens and disappears, the infant gradually learns to grasp objects voluntarily – holding and shaking a rattle or a toy. With time, she refines this grasp, enabling her to pick up and manipulate tiny objects with her finger tips.

Another striking primitive reflex that has to be lost as the child grows is the asymmetric tonic neck reflex. With this reflex, if the baby's head turns to one side, her arm and, to a lesser extent, her leg on that side extend, while her arm on the other side flexes, so she takes up a kind of fencing posture.

We can see the devastating effect of a persistence of this reflex in some children with cerebral palsy. If these children turn their heads to look at something, their arms will automatically take up this fencing posture, making it very difficult for them to coordinate their vision and manipulation. In contrast, most children, as they lose this reflex, learn to focus their vision on objects, then move their hands out to reach and grasp, starting with objects immediately in front of them and gradually enlarging their fields of influence. Simultaneously they learn to judge distance and position. As they do so, the process opens up a whole new world of possibilities.

Imprinting

Another amazing aspect of development is that all these new tasks the young child learns become imprinted in her brain, so she does not have to relearn a task each time she does it. You no longer need to think about how to stand or walk or hold a pencil – the patterns for these actions are all there in your brain. The old primitive reflexes have been replaced by new reflex actions.

Imprinting isn't limited to basic survival tasks, but can also extend to far more complex tasks, like learning to touch type on a keyboard or learning to play an instrument. Clearly, as you start out, you need to practice, and in order to stay proficient and develop, you need to keep practicing. But by doing so, the task becomes instinctive.

When you were first starting to learn the piano, my wonderful daughter, you had to think carefully about which finger to place on which key to produce which note. Now, if you play a two-octave scale on the piano, you no longer need to think about moving your fingers across the keys, tucking your thumb under as your hand glides up the keyboard. It just happens.

Bumps and bruises

As the child grows and gains strength, we have seen how her increasing mobility takes place in the context of developing protective reflexes. Her ability to step out and explore is matched by intrinsic protections carefully designed to minimise the chances of her causing herself harm. Of course, these are not absolute protections. The young toddler learning to walk will fall. She will fall repeatedly. She will get bumps and bruises. Learning to walk is not all plain sailing.

So it is in our spiritual walk. We will stumble and fall. We will get bruised. But we can be assured that God has put in place safeguards to prevent us from being seriously wounded. He will not expect or allow us to walk or run before we can stand. Paul, in his first letter to the Corinthians, tells us, 'No temptation has seized you except what is common to man. And God is faithful; he will not let you be tempted beyond what you can bear. But when you are tempted, he will also provide a way out so that you can stand up under it.'[71]

---

[71]   1 Corinthians 10:13.

Muscle tone

As a paediatrician, I am often referred young children who are delayed in their development, including those who are slow in learning to walk. Sometimes there is a genuine underlying medical disorder preventing them from acquiring those skills. These children typically fall into one of two broad groups: those with low muscle tone (hypotonia) and those with high muscle tone (hypertonia).

Children with hypotonia have weak, floppy muscles which are unable to support their weight effectively. We find this, for example, in children with Down syndrome. Those with hypertonia, such as children with some forms of cerebral palsy, have stiff, inflexible muscles. They find it equally difficult to walk, but for different reasons: their muscles, though stiff, are still weak, and they cannot easily achieve the coordination and balance to stand upright.

When I am assessing a young child's ability to stand and walk, I need to provide him with support and a stable base so he feels secure. In order to do this, I typically sit or kneel on the floor, with the child sitting between my legs, his back to me. When the child is sitting like that, he feels secure and safe. Those with high muscle tone often relax, enabling me to move their legs and assess the muscle strength.

Once I have the child properly relaxed, I will gently lift him to a more upright position, his trunk still supported against me, my arms around him, keeping him from falling. In that position, the child can feel secure and is able to take some weight on his legs, perhaps even taking some preliminary, supported steps.

I often think of God being like that with me. In my spiritual development, I may feel weak and hypotonic, unable to stand up in the face of difficult challenges. Or I may try too hard, my hypertonic spiritual muscles getting in the way of my attempts to go forward. I may feel insecure and afraid of falling or getting things wrong, or I may have already been hurt by life's events and be feeling a bit bruised and battered. In all those situations, I picture God as a heavenly paediatrician, holding me securely in his embrace, giving me the strength and courage to take those first, tentative steps.

That is the picture conveyed by Hosea's passionate words of God's love for the people of Israel: 'It was I who taught Ephraim to walk, taking them by the arms'.[72] God is someone we can trust, who will not let us fall. Secure in God's loving embrace, we can step out, even into the hardest of situations.

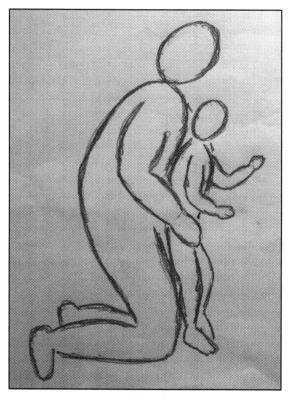

It was I who taught Ephraim to walk

---

[72]   Hosea 11:3.

Bottom shufflers

But we need to take those steps. Often, with children I assess for developmental delay, there is no underlying medical problem. It is simply that they are taking longer than other children to get there.

One of the commonest reasons for this delay is children who, instead of learning to walk, are quite happy shuffling about on their bottoms. These 'bottom-shufflers' can sometimes get about at incredible speeds. They are quite content being able to explore their world from the secure base of their bottoms. Why bother to stand up and risk getting hurt if you can get about satisfactorily on your bottom?

We, in our spiritual lives, may be similar. We are content to stay on our bottoms, accepting a gentle and non-threatening spirituality. But God doesn't want us to stay there. He wants us to stand, to walk, to run. We need to take the risk. We need to step out and accept the falls and bumps that brings, secure in the knowledge of God's overarching love for us.

And, like a young toddler learning to walk, when we do fall over, we don't need to stay there. God gives us both the ability and the motivation to get up and walk again.

Developing new reflexes

Just as a baby needs to lose the inherent primitive reflexes she is born with, we need to set aside those reflex actions that get in the way of the spiritual development God wants us to achieve.

Like the grasp reflex, we as humans have deep-seated, inherent reactions to situations we may face. We think first of ourselves, acting for our own comfort or security. We experience worries that prevent us trusting God and greed that makes us grasp and hold on to things. All of these are very strong, 'natural' human characteristics. But we know that they are not of God's kingdom. We need to 'unlearn' or lay down these reactions in order to take on the new and radical values of Jesus's kingdom.

Our instinct is to worry about things. Jesus tells us, 'Do not worry about your life, what you will eat or drink, or about your body, what you will wear.'[73] Our instinct is to fight back if someone abuses us. Jesus tells us to 'turn the other cheek'[74] and to 'love your enemies and pray for those who persecute you'.[75] Our instinct is to stand up for our rights. Jesus tells us to 'walk the extra mile'.[76] Our instinct is to save and store up for our security. Jesus tells us to 'store up for yourselves treasures in heaven'.[77] Our instinct is to judge others. Jesus tells us to 'take the plank out of your own eye'.[78] Our instinct is to hang out with those we get on with. Jesus tells us, 'If you love those who love you, what reward will you get? ... And if you greet only your own people, what are you doing more than others?'[79] Jesus got alongside those who were needy, looked down on, and excluded, and he calls us to do the same.

Evolutionary theory emphasises the survival of the fittest. It is perhaps 'natural' for us to think and act first for ourselves – to secure our own survival. It seems that what Jesus came to do was to overturn this 'natural' order and suggest, instead a new, more powerful, 'supernatural' order – one that is based not so much on survival of the fittest, but on humility, vulnerability, and compassion for the least.

So, in following Jesus and becoming like a child, we lay down our primitive, 'natural' instincts and instead learn new ways of being, taking on Jesus's way of relating to others, of trusting God,

---

[73]   Matthew 6:25.
[74]   Matthew 5:39.
[75]   Matthew 5:44.
[76]   Matthew 5:41.
[77]   Matthew 6:20.
[78]   Matthew 7:5.
[79]   Matthew 5:46–47.

of caring for the Creator's world. As we practice these new ways of behaving, they too will gradually become instinctive. Like learning to walk or talk or play the piano, these patterns of behaviour can become imprinted in our lives so that they replace the original patterns with new instincts.

6

MIND

Mental Development

Do not conform any longer to the pattern of this world,
but be transformed by the renewing of your mind.

- Romans 12:2

I am not a psychologist, and my understanding of cognitive development is limited. Nevertheless I find this one of the most fascinating aspects of human development. It is one of the key characteristics that distinguishes us from other animals. Descartes famously stated *'cogito, ergo sum'*: 'I think, therefore I am.' While it is not the sum of our being, our ability to think, to reason, is one of our defining characteristics. Mostly this aspect of development is hidden, but it perhaps progresses more dramatically than any other. I will explore just some aspects of it, recognising that others are better qualified to expound on the full breadth of a child's mental development.

Naming

One of the first signs of mental development is our ability to name things. This is partly tied in with language development, which I shall explore in more detail in the next chapter. But I think it is more than just a tool for communication. Naming things is a prerequisite for us to reason, to remember, and to identify patterns. Most of us think, at least in part, with language. It is interesting that the biblical account of creation assigns naming as one of the first tasks man undertakes: '[The Lord God] brought [all the beasts of the field and the birds of the air] to the man to see what he would name them; and whatever the man called each living creature, that was its name.'[80]

My dear Esther, some of my fondest memories of you relate to your developing vocabulary as you grew. One of the first words you learned to say, when you were eleven months old, was 'gecko'. We were living in Cambodia at the time, and you were fascinated by these little creatures as they scuttled across the walls and ceiling. You would point excitedly at them ('proto-declarative' pointing – more on that later), proudly saying your new word. I'm not sure if you were discovering your true human vocation, following in the footsteps of Adam in giving names to all the animals, but certainly 'duck', 'fly', 'tito' (mosquito), 'hop' (frog), and others soon followed.

After your first year, you rapidly gained a huge vocabulary, going from seemingly meaningless babble, through individual words for familiar people and objects, to dozens and then hundreds of words for a whole host of people, objects and places. Nouns were followed by verbs, adjectives, comparators, and more abstract concepts. This naming process allowed you to understand and bring order to your world, and thereby to gain some control over it.

Object permanence

Memory plays an important part in our learning, and it also develops as we grow. For the very young infant, memory is limited, and her experience is probably very much bounded by the present.

---

[80] Genesis 2:19.

We see this in the way a baby handles toys. There is a wonderful, short phase in development during which the infant has learned the skills necessary to reach out and grasp objects with either hand, but has not yet learned the concept of 'object permanence' – that is, the understanding that objects continue to exist even when they are not immediately apparent.

If you hand a wooden brick to a baby around the age of six months, she will reach out and grasp it in her hand. If you hand her a second brick, she will usually reach out and grasp it in her other hand. If you then hand her a third brick, she will 'forget' about one of the other bricks, reach out to grab the new one, and drop the first on the way. It is very consistent, predictable, and amusing to watch. A month or so later, she will have moved beyond this, and will either try and hold two bricks in one hand, not bother with the new one, or, if it seems more exciting, take the new one, but more deliberately drop the first in order to do so.

This concept of object permanence gives rise to one of the world's most exciting games for a baby towards the end of her first year of life: dropping a toy and expecting her mum or dad to pick it up again. She knows that when she drops the toy, it continues to exist. She also knows that she is the centre of the world and that she wants that toy back again. So, patiently, with a smile and a playful reprimand, her mother will pick the toy up and give it to her again, only to have her throw it on the floor once more. Parents can be so gullible.

Pattern recognition

Another crucial aspect of our cognitive development is pattern recognition. Young children love matching things. Whether it is fitting a circular shape in a form-board, matching colours on a colour chart, or using more complex shape sorters, puzzles, and pictures, the child learns to recognise patterns in the world around her. In time this same pattern recognition extends to language patterns, concepts of time and space, mathematical patterns, and the intricacies of science and art. It seems to be an inherent part of our nature that we seek out pattern and order in the world around us. We expect the world to make some sense and so search for the sense that we believe is there.

This ability to recognise patterns allows the growing child to understand concepts of cause and effect. It also allows her to predict things, including the consequences of her own and others' actions. This can then lead to modifications in her behaviour in order to achieve desired consequences. When you were about fifteen months old, Esther, you had grasped principles of cause and effect and decided to teach that to your cuddly toys: 'Be careful, Panda, 'cos this is the wobbly one [stool], and you have to sit in the middle carefully, carefully, not on the edge like this, just in the middle.'

Sometimes you got confused about the whole process of cause and effect. Your understanding of logic could be a bit muddled: 'My hair is dirty 'cos it needs washing.' 'The children are sick in "hosserbul" 'cos Daddy's looking after them.'

At first your understanding of cause and effect tended to be very self-centred: if I shake this rattle, it will make a nice sound which will please me. In time it extended beyond yourself to pleasing others: if I give my mum a bunch of flowers, I know she will be pleased.

To some extent children also seek to impose order and pattern where there is none. This isn't always immediately apparent, but is perhaps most clearly seen in autistic children. Typically these children have a heightened need for order in their environment. Thus they like things to always follow predictable patterns, to the extent that they may rebel if there is a change in their usual routines. Interestingly, this can help explain some of the behaviour traits we see in such children. When they perceive their world as being disordered or unpredictable, they will often resort to behaviours which to them are ordered and predictable, such as spinning objects, throwing tantrums, or even hurting themselves. With all these activities, they know what will happen and what it will feel like.

Pattern recognition is the basis for most scientific and mathematical endeavour. As humans we look for rules and patterns in our world, describe those rules, and then test them through scientific experiments.

Reasoning

This leads us to a further and more complex area of mental development, that of reasoning. This quality seems to develop at a relatively late stage, and involves the child understanding and thinking through not just concrete things that she can immediately observe, but increasingly more abstract concepts.

We see this in the progression of the questions children ask and in their use of language. In the early stages, a young child's language consists of single words, mostly involving people and familiar objects. She learns to ask 'what?' to learn to identify and name things, then 'where?' to seek things out. The 'what' question then extends to activities: 'What are you doing?' As she learns concepts of time, she starts asking 'when?' At a similar time, she asks the most profound question of all: 'why?'

By the age of about four, this questioning is one of the most consistent, distinguishing characteristics of children. It may drive their parents to distraction, but it underlies a deep-seated desire to explore, to learn about, and to seek to understand their world.

Redeeming our minds

When he calls us to become like little children, I do not think Jesus is asking us to set aside our minds. They are an integral part of what it means to be human. Rather than dispensing with our reason in some kind of mindless faith, I believe God wants to redeem, use, and develop our minds just as a young child will do as she grows.

We see hints of this throughout the Bible, perhaps no more clearly than in the injunctions, in the Psalms and elsewhere, to remember:

> I will remember the deeds of the Lord; yes, I will remember your miracles of long ago.[81]

> Remember the wonders he has done, his miracles, and the judgments he pronounced.[82]

Memory, both individual and collective, serves as a basis for our faith in God. We remind ourselves of God's goodness, what we have experienced of that, and what we are told of it through others and through God's Word. It strikes me also that God wants us to seek out patterns:

> When I look at the heavens, even the work of your fingers,
> the moon and the stars majestic in their courses ...
> who are we human beings that you keep us in mind,
> children, women, and men that you care so much
> for us?[83]

God wants us to remember, to seek patterns in creation, and to create order in this world – to be part of an ongoing work of creation. 'The Lord God took the man and put him in the Garden of Eden to work it and take care of it.'[84]

God-permanence

I think that one of the most profound aspects of our becoming like a child is that we need to learn the concept of 'God permanence'.

---

[81]   Psalm 77:11.

[82]   1 Chronicles 16:12.

[83]   Psalm 8, *Psalms for a pilgrim people*, 13.

[84]   Genesis 2:15.

A young infant doesn't have an understanding of object permanence and so will not know that the toy she has been playing with continues to exist even when she stops playing with it. More profoundly, at the earliest stage she does not know that her mother continues to exist when she can't see, feel, or hear her. When her mother puts her down and leaves her, she has no guarantee that this same mother will come back. She soon learns, however, that her mother is faithful. Although she may at times doubt it when her mother doesn't immediately come, she learns that it is OK.

As adults, we cannot conceive what it is like not to have that understanding, or how it must feel for an infant without the deep-seated assurance of her mother's constancy. But this is very similar to our relationship with God. We have no certainty that God actually exists. No matter how profoundly we may experience God at times, we cannot guarantee that he really is there. This is where faith comes in.

A poem, allegedly found written on a wall somewhere in Germany after the fall of the Berlin Wall, captures this faith beautifully:

> I believe in the sun, even when it is not shining;
> I believe in love, even when I feel it not;
> I believe in God, even when he is silent.[85]

This is not just a blind faith. It is a faith that draws on our reason rather than setting it aside. It is a faith that is prepared to question. Like the young child, we ask questions and challenge God.

I think that our deepest questions come down to four main issues: where we came from, why we are here, where we are going, and why there is so much suffering. Perhaps all four are interconnected. The epitome of this questioning is in the book of Job, where we see Job addressing all four of these issues. In the Psalms too we see the

---

[85] www.searchquotes.com/ Accessed 16.5.14

psalmist time and time again question God. It is as though God is encouraging us to question, to probe, and to challenge.

Wisdom

As a child grows, she gains knowledge and understanding. However, I think we see in Scripture that God wants our mental development to go even further, to a higher plane. Beyond knowledge and understanding comes wisdom. That wisdom is, in a sense, a gift from God that transcends human mental ability. In a way, our becoming like a child paves the way for God to grant us wisdom.

We see this in the humility shown by Solomon when God presented him with the opportunity to ask for whatever he wanted. Solomon answered, 'I am only a little child and do not know how to carry out my duties … so give your servant a discerning heart to govern your people and to distinguish between right and wrong.'[86] Or, in the Chronicles version, 'Give me wisdom and knowledge, that I may lead this people.'[87]

God wants us to seek wisdom:

> Get wisdom, get understanding;
> do not forget my words or swerve from them.
> Do not forsake wisdom, and she will protect you;
> love her, and she will watch over you.
> Wisdom is supreme; therefore get wisdom.
> Though it cost all you have, get understanding.

---

[86]   1 Kings 3:7–9.

[87]   2 Chronicles 1:10.

Esteem her, and she will exalt you;
embrace her, and she will honour you.[88]

The starting point for this wisdom is having a right relationship with God: 'The fear of the Lord is the beginning of wisdom.'[89] I am sure this isn't fear in a negative, terrifying sense, but fear in a deep, reverent, loving, and awesome way: that of a young child, who loves her father and mother and trusts them implicitly to take care of her.

In that wonderful passage in Matthew's gospel, Jesus invites us all: 'Come to me, all you who are weary and burdened, and I will give you rest. Take my yoke upon you and learn from me, for I am gentle and humble in heart, and you will find rest for your souls. For my yoke is easy and my burden is light.'[90] We all need that rest, and we can find it by coming to Jesus as little children, trusting in him and resting in his love.

Wisdom is a gift from God, and one to be sought above all others. In the most profound way, attaining this wisdom comes through becoming like a child. I think this has something to do with opening our eyes to see God's kingdom.

In another puzzling passage, Jesus prayed, 'I praise you, Father, Lord of heaven and earth, because you have hidden these things from the wise and learned, and revealed them to little children.'[91] This prayer comes straight after Jesus has highlighted the signs of his kingdom: 'The blind receive sight, the lame walk, those who have leprosy are cured, the deaf hear, the dead are raised, and the good news is preached to the poor.'[92] Jesus suggests that children could see these signs of his kingdom, whereas those who purported to be wise couldn't. As adults, we too often lose that ability to see the world, as young children do, through God's eyes.

---

[88]   Proverbs 4:5–8.
[89]   Proverbs 1:7.
[90]   Matthew 11:28–30.
[91]   Matthew 11:25.
[92]   Matthew 11:5.

Attentiveness

Learning to see God's kingdom like little children requires us to pause and become attentive to the world around us. We must be attentive to God's creation – its beauty, its life, its power, its pain – and to those around us – to see God in each person. Too often, in our busy lives, we lose that attentiveness, and our sight becomes dull or distorted. The writer Esther de Waal expresses this powerfully:

> We need to hear again Christ's very simple command: "Come and *see*." I guess that we all know only too well how easily, and often how imperceptibly, the lens with which we view the world can become dull and lifeless. We need to take time to adjust the focus and ask ourselves if we might not have a distorting lens.[93]

Over the past few years, I have rediscovered the importance of taking time to adjust my focus. For me, this has involved a process of slowing down, of pausing. It has involved taking time to still myself, to become attentive to myself, to the world around me, and to God. Poetry, art, walks in the countryside – all of these can help us to see more clearly. But most of all, we need to be still.

---

[93]   E. de Waal. *Lost in wonder*. Norwich, UK: Canterbury Press, 2003, 2.

7

HEART

Social Development

Come near to God and He will come near to you.

- James 4:8

The way a young child develops her language skills is quite incredible. Indeed, the very concept of language is astounding – that we can use vocal symbolic representation to portray the world around us and to communicate that representation with others in a meaningful and purposeful way.

There are two core sides to language development: comprehension and expression. While expressive language development is the most obvious (we can hear a young child's attempts to make noises and speak, but we can't immediately hear or see what goes on in her head as she hears others speak), as a general rule comprehension tends to be just a little ahead of expression. The two, however, develop hand in hand in an intricate, reciprocal dance. In fact, while comprehension may lead, I think it is probably expression that makes the first move.

The young infant initially communicates primarily by crying and other, non-verbal forms of communication. As she goes through her first few months, however, she gradually starts making a range of different vocalisations: coos, gurgles, laughs. These form themselves into different vowel sounds, which become repeated and interspersed with simple, separating consonants to form polysyllabic babble.

It is around this stage that the prominence of comprehension comes in. The baby has already learned, very early, to turn to sound, then specifically to turn to the sound of her parents' voices. Increasingly she seems to recognise that the sounds coming from her parents carry some meaning. First she recognises her own name, then the names of other people, and then the names of common objects – bath, cup, bed, gecko. As she learns to recognise her mother and other people saying these words, and to associate them with the objects they represent, her ability to formulate a range of different sounds is also developing. Eventually she starts to be more precise in forming words herself and relating them to the objects she is naming.

From there, her language development takes off exponentially. She learns that words can go together to express actions ('Daddy gone'), then descriptions, then increasingly complex ideas. She learns to understand simple instructions and to identify objects just from the words said.

Alongside this, her speech also becomes more and more sophisticated. From single, isolated words, she starts putting words together, then forming simple phrases and sentences. Eventually she learns to carry out whole conversations. At first, this language is focused on concrete ideas in her physical world – the nature and location of people and objects. As time goes on, however, her language moves from description to explanation to ever more abstract and complex notions – feelings, consequences, predictions, hypothetical situations.

Intriguingly, although it is the adults who have the advantage here, already possessing highly developed language skills, it is in fact the baby who mostly takes the lead in this complex interplay. If you watch an adult interacting with a young baby, you will often see the baby firmly leading this interaction. Each time the baby smiles, the adult reacts with a smile of encouragement and wonderful cooing sounds. The baby makes a noise and immediately the adult makes a noise in response – a coo for a coo, a gurgle for a gurgle. With the adult copying back the baby's attempts to communicate, that communication develops. It is that reciprocation which is key to the development of communication. Unlike some other aspects of development, communication really cannot develop in isolation. Because, by its very nature, communication is interactive, it needs interaction to grow.

Attachment

My dear Esther, I said earlier that one of your first words was 'gecko'. It wasn't your first word though. In keeping with almost every other baby, the first recognisable word you managed to say consistently was 'Dada'. I wouldn't dream of concluding that there was any favouritism on your part, but it was at least another couple of months before you were saying 'Mumum' as enthusiastically.

It is significant that a baby's first words usually are names for her mother and father, and later for herself and other family members. Other objects, actions, and descriptions all come later. It is people who feature most prominently in a baby's early understanding and speech. Communication, at its heart, is all about relationship, and first and foremost about family relationships.

A child's social development goes far beyond the development of language to incorporate other aspects of relationship and social interaction. One of the most profound elements of this is what we refer to as 'attachment'. This phenomenon was first described by John Bowlby, a psychiatrist, in the 1950s.[94]

---

[94]   J. Bowlby. *Attachment and loss, vol. 1: attachment.* London: Hogarth Press, 1969.

In essence, attachment refers to a close emotional proximity between one person and another. We see this most clearly between a baby and her mother. The attachment bond provides security for the baby, along with emotional closeness that works both ways. Interestingly, attachment only really becomes significant in the context of separation. Indeed, the very purpose of attachment is to provide a secure base from which the developing child can explore the world; its ultimate goal is to enable independence. This is really quite important.

A young child who does not feel a strong, secure attachment to her mother (or another primary caregiver) will not feel able to step away from that base, and so will not learn to explore the world. In contrast, a baby who has a secure attachment relationship can launch out, confident that her mother will still be there if something goes wrong. The baby crawls away from her mother to explore. The moment the baby senses any threat, she scuttles back to the security of her mother. As time goes on, this attachment relationship is strengthened, and the baby ventures further and further afield, each time coming back to her mother if she starts feeling anxious or if anything threatens her. Eventually that security allows her to separate completely from her mother for prolonged periods of time, still confident that her mother will be there if she needs her.

Bowlby's work was built upon by another psychologist, Mary Ainsworth, to describe three main types of attachment behaviour: secure, anxious-avoidant, and anxious-ambivalent or resistant attachment. Mary Ainsworth demonstrated these with a neat little experiment called the 'strange situation'.

In this experiment, a mother and her young child are observed in the strange (to the baby) situation of a clinic room. They are left to play together for a while, during which time the mother will typically sit on the floor with the child, who enjoys playing with her mother and will crawl around and explore the room, happily knowing her mother is there. If another, unknown, adult enters the room, the infant may interact with that adult, provided the mother is present.

The mother is then asked to leave the room quietly. It may be a while before the baby notices this, as she continues to explore and play. Eventually, however, she notices that her mother is not in the room and starts to get distressed. This distress will continue, and indeed increase, until her mother returns to the room, after which the baby usually settles quickly as her mother comforts her. If another adult enters the room before the mother returns, the infant will not interact with the stranger and will not be comforted by them.

That, of course, is a typical, secure attachment – the baby becomes appropriately distressed when her mother is not there for her, but is quickly reassured when she returns. In contrast, a baby with an insecure attachment may fail to show any distress when her mother leaves the room, or may fail to be comforted when her mother returns.

Insecure attachment

In the context of a violent home environment, when the baby experiences physical or emotional abuse from her parents, she may develop anxious-avoidant attachment behaviour. Her parent ceases to be a source of reassurance and instead becomes a threat. The avoidant behaviour is adaptive and protective. Such children, however, tend to be somewhat passive; they do not explore widely, they tend not to show much in the way of different emotions, and they tend to treat strangers in a similar manner to their own parents.

A child with an anxious-ambivalent or resistant pattern of attachment tends to be very anxious about exploring and very wary of strangers, regardless of whether her mother is present or not. In contrast to an anxious-avoidant child, an anxious-ambivalent one will tend to get very distressed when her mother leaves. When her mother returns, she displays a curious mixture of emotional responses – turning to the mother for security and support, but at the same time showing resentment, and resisting any advances made by the mother.

What is interesting is that the attachment behaviour is primarily (though not exclusively, and there are some notable exceptions to this) dependent not so much on the baby, but on the mother's character and responses. The mother needs to be attuned to the baby's needs in order for a secure attachment relationship to develop. If the mother is not attuned, the baby will tend not to seek reassurance from her. Similarly if the response the baby gets from her mother varies, the attachment behaviour she develops may be disorganised, sometimes demonstrating one style and at other times another, never quite being sure what to expect from others.

Developing a secure attachment to God

I think God wants us to develop secure attachment relationships with him, and this is perhaps a part of what Jesus is calling us to when he tells us to become like little children. He wants us to be secure in the knowledge that God is there and is caring for us. From that base, he wants is to be able to step out confidently into the situations God places us in.

That, however, is dependent on God being attuned to us and demonstrating qualities that foster a secure attachment. Thus we need to know that God is faithful, that he will not change, that his attitude to us is caring and responsive, that he will neither harm us nor turn away from us when we turn to him, and that he will be there when we need him. It is amazing just how much of the Bible picks up on these very things.

- **God is faithful:** 'Know therefore that the Lord your God is God; he is the faithful God, keeping his covenant of love to a thousand generations of those who love him and keep his commands.'[95] 'Your steadfast love, O God, extends through the universe, your faithfulness to the furthest stars.'[96] 'God, who has called you into fellowship with his Son Jesus Christ our Lord, is faithful.'[97] 'But the Lord is faithful, and he will strengthen and protect you from the evil one.'[98]

- *God will not change:* 'He who is the glory of Israel does not lie or change his mind; for he is not a man that he should change his mind.'[99] 'I the Lord do not change.'[100] 'Every good and perfect gift is from above, coming down from the Father of the heavenly lights, who does not change like shifting shadows.'[101]

- *God's attitude to us is caring and responsive:* 'I cast my burden on you, O God, and you will sustain and encourage me.'[102] 'The Lord is good, a refuge in times of trouble. He cares for those who trust in him.'[103] 'Cast all your anxiety on him because he cares for you.'[104]

- *God will not harm us:* 'Which of you fathers, if your son asks for a fish, will give him a snake instead? Of if he asks for an egg, will give him a scorpion? If you then, though you are evil, know how to give good gifts to your children, how much more will your Father in heaven give the Holy Spirit to those who ask him!'[105]

---

[95]   Deuteronomy 7:9.
[96]   Psalm 36, *Psalms for a pilgrim people*, 77.
[97]   1 Corinthians 1:9.
[98]   2 Thessalonians 3:3.
[99]   1 Samuel 15:29.
[100]   Malachi 3:6.
[101]   James 1:17.
[102]   Psalm 55, *Psalms for a pilgrim people*, 117.
[103]   Nahum 1:7.
[104]   1 Peter 5:7.
[105]   Luke 11:11–13.

- **God will not turn away from us:** 'The Lord your God is gracious and compassionate. He will not turn his face from you if you return to him.'[106] 'This is what the Lord Almighty says: "Return to me," declares the Lord Almighty, "and I will return to you," says the Lord Almighty.'[107] 'Come near to God and he will come near to you.'[108]

- **God will be there when we need him:** 'Be strong and courageous. Do not be afraid or terrified … for the Lord your God goes with you; he will never leave you nor forsake you.'[109] 'Even when I go through the deepest valley, with the shadow of darkness and death, I will fear no evil or harm. For you are with me to give me strength, your crook, your staff, at my side.'[110] 'Gently you embrace the broken in heart, and revive the crushed in spirit.'[111]

Sadly, though, for many people, that is not their perception of God. And it is easy to understand why. Although the Bible talks of a God who is always there, he is not visibly present, and often we find it hard to sense his presence at all.

We can end up conceiving of God as an absent parent – a creator who set the world in motion, then left it to its own devices – or a non-emotional, uncaring intelligent-designer, or an impersonal force – a nebulous entity which resulted in the universe being as it is. Or we may say he is not there at all, a figment of human imaginations in an uncreated universe.

At the other extreme, and I suspect the Church may have a lot to answer for here, we may view God as a personal God, but a malicious, not a benevolent God. While I don't want to minimise the

---

[106] 2 Chronicles 30:9.

[107] Zechariah 1:3.

[108] James 4:8.

[109] Deuteronomy 31:6.

[110] Psalm 23, *Psalms for a pilgrim people*, 50.

[111] Psalm 34, *Psalms for a pilgrim people*, 73.

importance of God's judgement and justice, when that is emphasised above or before God's love and mercy, we can very easily end up with a distorted view of God. Instead of being a loving, caring parent, we perceive God to be a distant, cold judge, or worse still, a cruel tyrant who wants to inflict pain and suffering.

When our view of God is either of an absent, impersonal, and uncaring being, or of a cruel, unpredictable despot, we will not form the kind of secure attachment God intends us to have. Instead, we will find it really hard to come to God. We may anxiously avoid God; we may approach him hesitantly, unsure of how we will be received; we may blame God and accuse him for the way we perceive him to be; or we may try to bargain with him. All of these are marks of insecure attachment, and not what Jesus calls us to in asking us to become like little children.

Instead, Jesus calls us to approach God confidently, secure in the knowledge that he loves us. We can do this, not because of our own merit, but because of who God is, because of his faithful, loving nature. And we can do this because of what God has done through Jesus.

> In this way, love is made complete among us so that we will have confidence on the day of judgment, because in this world we are like him. There is no fear in love. But perfect love drives out fear, because fear has to do with punishment.[112]

> Let us then approach the throne of grace with confidence, so that we may receive mercy and find grace to help us in our time of need.[113]

> Therefore, brothers, since we have confidence to enter the Most Holy Place by the blood of Jesus,

---

[112]   1 John 4:17–18.

[113]   Hebrews 4:16.

by a new and living way opened for us through the curtain, that is, his body, and since we have a great priest over the house of God, let us draw near to God with a sincere heart in full assurance of faith, having our hearts sprinkled to cleanse us from a guilty conscience and having our bodies washed with pure water. Let us hold unswervingly to the hope we profess, for he who promised is faithful.[114]

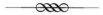

Learning to communicate with God

As we learn to approach God with confidence, from a place of secure attachment, we also start learning to communicate with God.

Learning to communicate with God, though, is not easy. We rely for communication on our senses – auditory, visual, tactile. Communication is not just speaking; it is listening as well, and a lot of it is non-verbal, relying on observing and on our expressions and actions.

But the reality is that we cannot see God and we do not hear God, at least not in the ways we are used to seeing and hearing. No wonder the psalmist cries out:

> My God, my God, why have you forsaken me? Why are you so far from helping me? O my God, I howl in the daytime but you do not hear me. I groan in the watches of the night, but I find no rest.[115]

> I am worn out calling for help; my throat is parched. My eyes fail, looking for my God.[116]

---

[114] Hebrews 10:19–23.
[115] Psalm 22, *Psalms for a pilgrim people*, 43.
[116] Psalm 69:3.

Just as a young baby needs her mother to respond and look at her, so we need God to respond to us. Time and again the Israelites pleaded with God to 'let the light of your face shine upon us'.[117] We try to pray, but wonder if God even hears our prayers.

Learning to listen

So we need to learn afresh how to communicate with God. This has to start with learning to listen in new ways. It seems to me that this new way of listening doesn't come naturally. Over the years, we have laid down patterns of listening that don't leave space for hearing God. These patterns have become fixed in our brains and perhaps in our hearts and souls. Too many other things get in the way of our seeing or hearing God. So we need to become again like little children, allowing God to teach us new ways of listening and looking. We need to quieten ourselves and remove other distractions to allow God to speak to us in ways that we can hear.

The pattern of communication I described above relies on pauses. The baby may vocalise or make some expression, but then she stills herself, listens, and watches her mother for a reaction. We often seem to miss this in our prayers, in which we do all the talking but forget to pause and listen, to give God space to respond.

God doesn't shout to gain our attention. It seems to me that the Holy One communicates gently, in whispers. Rabbi Jonathan Sacks expresses this beautifully in a reflection on Elijah's encounter with God on Mount Horeb [118]:

> God tells Elijah to stand on the mountain, 'for the Lord is about to pass by.' Suddenly there is a great and powerful wind that tears the mountains apart and shatters the rocks. But God is not in the wind.

---

[117]   Psalm 4:6.
[118]   1 Kings 19.

Then there is an earthquake. But God is not in the earthquake. Then there is a fire. But God is not in the fire. After the fire comes a still, small voice. God is in that voice.

There are many ways of translating the Hebrew phrase for 'a still, small voice.' Some prefer 'a gentle whisper.' Others, more accurate to the original, render it 'the sound of a fine silence.' My own interpretation is different. What is a 'still, small voice'? It is a sound you can only hear if you are listening …

God does not impose Himself on His image, mankind. On the contrary, God – like a true parent – creates space for His children to grow. He is always there, but only if we seek Him. His word is always present, but only if we listen. Otherwise we do not hear it at all.

God is the music of all that lives, but there are times when all we hear is noise. The true religious challenge is to ignore the noise and focus on the music. The great command of the Bible, '*Shema Yisrael*,' does not mean, 'Hear, O Israel.' It means 'Listen.' Listening, we hear. Searching, we find.[119]

Learning to be still, to be silent and attentive, is a key part of becoming like a child. In a child's social development, comprehension comes before expression, listening before speaking. So often we tend to rush into God's presence with a lot of words, babbling away, bombarding the Holy One with our needs and desires, and never giving any space for God to speak to us. If we are to become like little children, we need to turn that round and learn instead to listen. That will take practice and presence.

---

[119]   J. Sacks. *Celebrating life*. London: Continuum, 2000, 74-75.

With that in mind, I want to finish this chapter – a chapter on communication – with a simple prayer from Esther de Waal[120]:

Uncrowd my heart, O God,
until silence speaks
in your still, small voice;
turn me from the hearing of words,
and the making of words,
and the confusion of much speaking,
to listening,
waiting,
stillness,
silence.

---

[120] E. de Waal. *Lost in wonder.* Norwich, UK: Canterbury Press, 2003, 42.

8

SOUL

Spiritual Development

*Praise the Lord, O my soul, and all that is
within me praise his holy name.*

- Psalm 103:1

In one of the episodes of the Dr Who television series, the Doctor's time machine, the Tardis, in human form (an intriguing incarnation!), looks into the Doctor's eyes and, with a sense of wonder in her voice, quietly asks, 'Are all people like this?'

'Like what?' asks the Doctor.

To which the Tardis replies, 'So much bigger on the inside.'

In that simple phrase, turned on its head as it were, the Tardis captures an incredible truth: we are bigger on the inside.

While I as a paediatrician, or my colleagues in clinical and developmental psychology may be able to observe, and to some extent understand, the processes of development taking place as a young child grows, there is always so much more that we can neither observe nor understand. This is true even in relation to some of the more straightforward aspects of physical, cognitive, and social development, but reaches incomparable depths when we consider our spiritual development. It is into those depths, my dear Esther, that I now want to cautiously delve, aware, as I do so, that there will always be so much I cannot possibly comprehend.

Once again the Psalms capture something of this incomprehensibility:

> For you have created every part of my being,
> cell, tissue, blood and bone.
> You have woven me in the womb of my mother;
> I will praise you, so wonderfully am I made ...
> You know me to the very core of my being;
> nothing in me was hidden from your eyes
> when I was formed in silence and secrecy,
> in intricate splendour in the depths of the earth.[121]

In attempting to describe something of our spiritual development, I recognise that I am straying into difficult and dangerous territory. There is so much I don't know or understand. Nevertheless, I think it is so crucial to our understanding of a child's development, of who we are, and of what it means to be born again and become like a little child that I do want to explore this and try to unravel some of the mystery of our spiritual development.

There is a second danger in this: that of setting our spiritual development apart as something that is somehow different and separate from all other aspects of our development. There is a risk of creating a sacred-secular divide that was never intended to be. I hope I have shown in the preceding chapters how our humanness is dependent on all aspects of our being: body, mind, heart, and soul. These four cannot be separated. Our spiritual development is worked out as much through our physical, cognitive, and social development as it is in any separate sphere. All of who we are is

---

[121] Psalm 139, *Psalms for a pilgrim people*, 305.

sacred: our bodies, our minds, our relationships. This is perhaps what the psalmist meant when he proclaimed, 'Praise the Lord, O my soul, and all my inmost being [or 'all that is within me'] praise his holy name.'[122]

A journey

In a sense our spiritual development is a journey, and one which I don't think we ever finish. While other aspects of our development may be largely (though not exclusively) confined to our childhood years, our spiritual development continues throughout our lives. It is a journey of discovery, a search for identity and meaning. As such it is a highly individual journey – your journey will not be the same as mine.

While I may be able to provide some pointers towards possible routes and destinations, I can neither determine nor describe the route and destination of your journey. These are largely (though again not exclusively) determined by your own choices and decisions.

While the ultimate destination may be open, I think the initial stages of this journey tend to be quite consistent and an integral part of our overall development. Primarily, I think this involves a growing awareness in four areas: awareness of self, awareness of others, awareness of creation, and awareness of God.

Awareness of self

A young child's awareness of herself begins at a very early stage. I suspect it starts with a social awareness, moving through physical and cognitive awareness to a more spiritual awareness. The young infant very quickly learns that her behaviour provokes reactions in

---

[122]   Psalm 103:1.

others. She smiles or coos, and her mother smiles and coos back; she cries, and she receives attention. This social awareness becomes increasingly complex as time goes on, but in its infant simplicity, I think it captures one of the keys of our identities: we were made to relate to and interact with others. First and foremost, we are relational beings.

A young infant also learns quickly that she has a body. This probably starts through her social awareness, as she learns that she can manipulate her face and vocal cords to initiate a response. It then, in keeping with other aspects of her development, moves downward. In some delightful moments, she recognises that her hands and then her feet are hers. It is wonderful watching this process of recognition. She starts by watching these objects waving about in front of her face, then gradually seems to realise that she has control over them, that she can move them about, put them into her mouth, play with them, and reach out to touch things with them.

Her cognitive awareness is most apparent later on, as she discovers the joys of naming, exploring, recognising patterns, playing, creating puzzles, and solving them. Young children love to use their minds as much as they love to use their bodies. They love to play and relate with others. Questions, memory games, and word play are all vital and fun parts of discovering the ability to think. Through these activities, the child develops an ever-increasing awareness of her own abilities and identity.

The questions a child asks give us some clues as to how her sense of identity is developing. She starts with a lot of 'what', 'where', and 'who' questions – identifying people and objects in her environment, discovering a sense of location, of who she is in relation to the world around her. These more factual, object-based questions lead to questions around activity.

Then there is a much deeper sense of identity that starts to kick in, with more profound 'why'-type questions. The child is trying to understand meaning and purpose. These questions point the child to her own sense of who she is.

Who am I?

One of the earliest of these questions most children ask is 'Where did I come from?' or 'Who made me?' This, of course, can be answered at the biological level, with convoluted explanations of Mummy's tummy and the great, embarrassed knots parents sometimes get into explaining about Mummy and Daddy loving each other very much, and how sometimes that results in some of Daddy getting into Mummy and joining together to make you!

I've no idea what youngsters really make of these muddled explanations, but at some point a child does gain an awareness that, in part, his or her identity comes from being the child of two parents. This sense of source is an important part of self-awareness.

Another important part of self-awareness is the sense of destiny: where am I going? Children seem to sense quite early on that they will not stay children forever. They engage in make-believe, constructing elaborate futures for themselves as mummies and daddies or doctors, nurses, police officers, princesses, astronauts, and so on.

As well as her past (source) and future (destiny), a child's growing identity is very firmly located in the present, with a growing sense of value and purpose. This is perhaps one of the most important, profound, and painful aspects of development in late childhood and adolescence. As she grows, she discovers her emotions, the things that delight and hurt her, and the things that make her tick. Increasingly, these aspects of her identity take on a shape of their own that is distinct from those of her parents.

I think this growing sense of identity is crucial to our understanding of what Jesus means when he tells us that we must become like little children.

I am not perfect

One important part of this is the growing awareness that I am not perfect. The journey of self-discovery isn't easy, and the child/adolescent has to cope with realising that neither the world around her nor her parents nor even she herself is perfect.

When a child starts gaining self-awareness, she does not have that sense of imperfection. The young infant or toddler sees herself as the centre of her world, adored by those around her, and rightly so. She may be aware of her limitations and may get frustrated by them, but she doesn't dwell on them or take them to heart.

With the teenage years come changes to her body, her emotions, and her social interaction, and with that, usually, a growing sense that she is not perfect. She may resent the spots that appear on her face, so often when she desperately wants to look perfect; she may likewise resent the even more inconvenient changes in her body shape and function. She realises that relationships don't last; friends fall out or get bitchy with each other. Then, typically, she struggles with the tensions of wanting to please herself and others, but finding that so often she doesn't.

The apostle Paul summed it up incredibly well in his letter to the Romans: 'I do not understand what I do. For what I want to do I do not do, but what I hate I do.'[123] I wonder how many teenagers have echoed those sentiments over the years. Paul locates these tensions in a recognition of sin: 'As it is, it is no longer I who do it, but it is sin living in me.'[124]

If we are to enter the kingdom of God, we need to recognise and acknowledge that we are not perfect; we too are sinners. This isn't just about acknowledging that we sometimes make mistakes or do things that are 'naughty'. It goes much deeper than that, in an adolescent recognition that there is something fundamentally wrong with us.

---

[123]   Romans 7:15.
[124]   Romans 7:17.

I can change

However, while we need to reach this point and acknowledge our imperfection, we mustn't stay there. In his interactions with others, Jesus, as with John the Baptist before him, places this recognition in the context of repentance, which implies turning round and heading in a different direction – moving on.

This is perhaps most clearly seen in Jesus's interaction with a woman caught in adultery.[125] Her accusers brought her before Jesus, threatening to stone her and asking for his views on what was right to do. She had many people accusing her, and I suspect was only too aware of her own imperfections – both her own guilt in relation to the act of adultery, but also as a victim, someone who was not valued or esteemed.[126]

Before saying anything to the woman, Jesus confronted her accusers with their own guilt: 'Let anyone of you who is without sin be the first to throw a stone at her.'[127] He confronted the culture that labelled people as sinners and condemned them with no opportunity for change.

When all her accusers had left, Jesus turned to the woman. He did not condemn her, but he made it clear that she could now change: 'Then neither do I condemn you …. Go now and leave your life of sin.'[128] That woman may or may not have had much choice in her own actions. Regardless of that, she stood condemned and unable to change. In one simple statement from Jesus, though, she was set free – not condemned as a sinner, but given the freedom to change, to become the person God had made her to be.

---

[125] John 8:3–11.

[126] We don't know any of the details of the adultery, but, as so often happens in our culture too, it was the woman and not the man who was blamed for this act. Her accusers labelled her a 'sinner'; they blamed her for her actions. What they did not see was the person within this woman.

[127] John 8:7

[128] John 8:11

I see a lot of adolescents who have got locked into a recognition of their own inadequacy and seem unable to get out of it. Often, though not invariably, this seems to happen in young people who have not received the loving affirmation they needed when they were younger.

While I think it is essential that we acknowledge (and repent of) our own failings and inadequacies, we can only truly do that from a basis of knowing that we are loved as we are, in spite of our sin, and that there is hope for us to change through the redeeming work of Jesus. Jesus does not condemn us to feelings of inadequacy or guilt. He offers the opportunity to change, for our true selves to shine through, creating the context for a new, redeemed life.

Seeing myself as God sees me

As I reflect on Jesus's invitation to us to become like little children, I wonder if this is an invitation to develop a redeemed self-awareness. Perhaps Jesus is inviting us to start seeing ourselves as God sees us: not as inadequate, messed-up sinners, condemned and trapped because we can never be good enough, but as beautiful, beloved children who can be set free and can change.

It troubles me that Christians have tended to focus so much on emphasising our sinfulness and God's judgement, without locating that firmly within the context of God's prior, unconditional love. In a very thoughtful exploration of children's spiritual development, Francis Bridger pointed out that children need 'a gospel of cuddles and softly spoken words'.[129]

---

[129]   F. Bridger. *Children finding faith*. London: Scripture Union, 1988, 22.

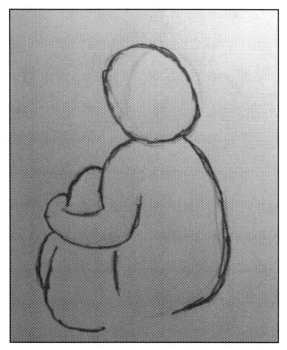

A gospel of cuddles and softly spoken words

I think the same applies to us all. Rather than condemning people with the 'good news' of their guilt and God's judgement and wrath, our starting point should be in demonstrating that they are individuals who are of worth, who are created and loved by God, and who can break free from the mess they find themselves in. Only then will they have the resilience and hope to turn to God in repentance.

Awareness of others

As a child grows, her social world slowly expands. Starting with her parents, it encompasses other family members and family friends, then children and teachers at nursery and school. In all of this the child will be relating and interacting with others, as we have seen in the previous chapter.

In the context of the child's growing identity and her spiritual development, awareness of others extends beyond the boundaries of social interaction to encompass the way the child perceives other people. An important part of this growing awareness is the development of empathy. At its root, empathy is the ability to see things from another's perspective, to put oneself in someone else's shoes.

Empathy

One aspect of this ability, the more cognitive side of it, relates to a concept called 'theory of mind'. Most children seem to develop this capacity around 5 to 7 years of age.

There is a neat little test that psychologists use to demonstrate whether a child has this understanding. My favourite version of this test uses an opaque box of chocolates and a pen. I first of all show the child the chocolates in the box and ask him what is in it. He will appropriately answer, 'chocolates'. I then ask him what he thinks his mother would say if I ask her what is in the box. Again he will correctly answer, 'chocolates'.

Then comes the fun bit. I ask the mother to leave the room; and while she is out, empty all the chocolates into another container, giving the child one to maintain his motivation. In place of the chocolates, I put a pen. I then ask the child what is in the box. He should answer, 'A pen.'

When I ask him what he thinks his mother will say when she comes back in, the response will vary depending on how developed his theory of mind is. A young child, or one without this capacity, will answer, 'A pen'. An older child who has developed a theory of mind will correctly answer, 'chocolates'. I then call his mother back, check her response, and share out the chocolates to great delight all round.

While this test will help determine whether a child has the cognitive ability to understand what another person might think, it does not truly capture what I mean by empathy. In fact, I think that children start to develop empathy a lot earlier than they develop a theory of mind.

In a way, children's spiritual development in this area advances more rapidly than their cognitive development. Even very young infants pick up on other people's emotions, and young children seem to sense how to respond to others' emotions very easily. When others are happy or enthusiastic, young children catch this enthusiasm and join in with great joy. When others are upset, they too become upset and seek to give comfort. This seems to come quite naturally to them.

All too often, as we grow, we block out others' emotions, particularly the painful ones. We don't want others' feelings to intrude on ours, so we learn to ignore them. We are cautious about getting too close to other people in case we get hurt.

This is spiritual development in the wrong direction. Ultimately it leads to a hardening of our hearts, so that we find it increasingly difficult to respond to others. We shut ourselves in, in an attempt to protect ourselves from the pain that relationships so often bring. In the words of Paul Simon's song:

> And a rock feels no pain,
> And an island never cries.[130]

Only it isn't true. We are made for love, and loneliness itself brings pain. So it seems we can't escape it. The poet John Donne was much closer to the truth when he said, 'No man is an island, Entire of itself.'[131]

---

[130] Paul Simon. 'I am a rock'. 1965.
[131] John Donne. 'Meditation XVII'. www.online-literature.com/donne/409/ Accessed 20.5.14

Our awareness of others, as part of our true spiritual development, involves recognition that we are part of humankind, that others are important. This needs to extend beyond our circle of family and friends. In one sense it is easy to develop empathy for those to whom we are close. After all, we get something back from them. But in another sense, even this isn't easy. It seems that our natural tendency is to be selfish; we tend to think of ourselves and our needs first. Empathy comes slowly and with difficulty.

The young child gradually learns to share, to take turns, to recognise the impact her actions will have on other people. But it is a painful journey, and one that certainly doesn't come naturally. As a father, Esther, I would get very upset when you or your brother Joseph acted selfishly. This tended to upset me more than any other misdemeanour. But you have learned and grown in this. And while you may not always live it out consistently (do any of us?), you do show an amazing ability to appreciate and respond to the needs of others.

Responding to injustice

Another stage in this aspect of our spiritual development is a growing awareness of those beyond our immediate social world. Children come to recognise that there is a world around them. They gain social and political awareness and a sense of right and wrong.

With this comes awareness of suffering – that there is a world out there where people are hurting; where children die every day for lack of food, clean water, or basic health care; where soldiers and civilians are killed or maimed through war; where whole communities are wiped out through natural disasters. And closer to home, a child develops awareness that there are people suffering through illness, children growing up in poverty, elderly people abandoned and alone, and people who are homeless, addicted, or mentally ill. Suffering is a stark reality of our world wherever we are.

Our response to this realisation can lead us in different directions. We can try to block it out, pretending it doesn't concern us and hardening our hearts to the injustice inherent in that. Or we can allow ourselves to be touched by it. If we let it, this growing awareness of the suffering in the world can lead to two rising emotions: anger and compassion.

I have already shown how I think that children gain a sense of empathy early on, and how this leads them to comfort others when they are hurt. I think children also gain a sense of justice at a very early stage, and this, channelled appropriately, becomes a healthy form of anger.

Even very young children soon learn to cry out, 'It's not fair!' Although this sentiment tends initially to be expressed on her own account, particularly when a child feels wronged by her brother or her parents, I think children naturally tend to extend this to others. So, while children may participate in perpetrating injustices on other children, they also are quick to realise when other children are suffering injustice.

What is needed in our spiritual development is the capacity to respond to that awareness, to speak out on behalf of, and to act with care towards those who are suffering injustice – both those on our doorstep and those further afield.

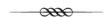

Justice and compassion

There is an incredible challenge here. If we are to truly develop spiritually, the way God wants us to develop, we need to go beyond our natural tendency to put ourselves first and to shield ourselves from the suffering around us. We need, rather, to recognise both suffering and oppression, to allow this recognition to lead to attitudes of anger and compassion, and to allow those attitudes to spill over into acts of justice and mercy. The Bible seems quite unequivocal in this.

Micah tells us that God requires us 'to act justly and to love mercy'.[132] Isaiah challenges us that the kind of fasting God has chosen is 'to loose the chains of injustice and untie the cords of the yoke, to set the oppressed free and to break every yoke'; it is 'to share your food with the hungry and to provide the poor wanderer with shelter – when you see the naked to clothe him'.[133] Jeremiah describes God as 'the Lord, who exercises kindness, justice and righteousness on earth, for in these I delight.'[134] The Old Testament is packed full with exhortations to God's people to act with justice and compassion.

Jesus himself repeatedly stresses his desire that we should care for the needy, perhaps nowhere more powerfully than in the parable of the sheep and goats. It is interesting that Jesus links this compassion for the poor and suffering with entry into his kingdom:

> Come, you who are blessed by my Father; take your inheritance, the kingdom prepared for you since the creation of the world. For I was hungry and you gave me something to eat, I was thirsty and you gave me something to drink, I was a stranger and you invited me in, I needed clothes and you clothed me, I was sick and you looked after me, I was in prison and you came to visit me.[135]

It seems to me that there is therefore a strong link between becoming like little children and developing a right spiritual awareness of and response to others. This comes with the promise of entering into God's kingdom.

---

[132] Micah 6:8.

[133] Isaiah 58:6, 7.

[134] Jeremiah 9:24.

[135] Matthew 25:34–36.

Awareness of creation

A friend of ours, who runs a children's group at our church, came up with a wonderful description of 3 to 6-year-olds: an age of 'awe and wonder'.

This sense of wonder begins very early, and I think it is one of the most delightful characteristics of young children. We can see something of this in the way infants use pointing. Typically, infant pointing is described as either 'imperative' or 'declarative'.[136]

Imperative pointing seems to develop first, and is geared towards achieving something. An infant who is thirsty will learn to point to her bottle; if she sees a biscuit or a toy that she wants, she will point to it. The aim of this imperative pointing is that the adult will give her what she wants.

Declarative pointing is altogether different and seems to reflect a desire to involve the other. This is the kind of pointing seen when a young infant points to a bus or a tree, or when you, Esther, as a young toddler in Asia, used to point to geckos as they scuttled across the ceiling. It is, in a sense, an attempt by the infant to share the wonder they feel. It is highly relational.

Appreciating beauty

While it may get damped down a bit with age, this sense of wonder at creation remains with us. We see it expressed in our desire to share beauty with others. When we see a stunning sunset or any other lovely view, we often want to share it with someone else.

I think that this wonder very naturally leads to praise. Throughout the Psalms, we see the psalmist looking to creation

---

[136] There is, perhaps, a third important type of pointing that children use: 'interrogative' (or inquisitive), the pointing they use when they want to discover something. 'What's that?' This type of pointing reflects the 'exploration' aspect of our development, which I will cover in the next chapter.

and bursting forth in praise; indeed he seems to feel that the whole of creation is joining in that song of praise, or perhaps that he, one person, is joining in the far greater song of praise that is continually rising up before God:

> Let the heavens rejoice, let the earth be glad;
> let the sea resound and all that is in it.
> Let the fields be jubilant, and everything in them;
> let all the trees of the forest sing for joy.
> Let all creation rejoice before the Lord.[137]

And the psalmist himself seems to recognise that this praise is nowhere more clearly expressed than by infants and children:

> O Lord, our Lord,
> how majestic is your name in all the earth!
> You have set your glory above the heavens.
> From the lips of children and infants
> you have ordained praise.[138]

This sense of awe and wonder develops very early in children, but, as with all other aspects of their nature, needs to grow and develop. I think we, as humans, have an incredible capacity for wonder. As the child grows, she will discover much more of the beauty of the world around her. She will learn to recognise and appreciate her likes and dislikes. Sights, sounds, smells, tastes – all of these go to form her appreciation of the world.

Art and music are two expressions of this in which children seem to engage instinctively. Young children love to draw. As soon as they can get their hands on crayons, they will start scribbling, gradually building on what they draw to form representations of the beauty

---

[137] Psalm 96:11–13.
[138] Psalm 8:1–2.

they see in the world. Young children also love to join in music, from simple nursery rhymes to the harmonies of a choir.

Perhaps part of what it means to become like a little child is to recapture some of that sense of awe and wonder: to appreciate the beauty around us, and ultimately to attribute praise to the Creator of that beauty.

As adults we often seem to crowd out the beauty in our lives, replacing beauty with business and brokenness. Our lives become so full of activity that we find little time to stop and appreciate beauty. Or we find ourselves crushed and overwhelmed by all the sadness and pain of our lives that we fail to recognise the beauty that is still there.

Living in the present

Becoming like a child involves discovering again that the world is 'wonder-filled'. The writer Esther de Waal explores that concept in her book of reflections, *Lost in wonder*. She encourages us to cultivate an attentiveness that opens us up to God's presence: 'I know how *vital* it is, using that word in its full implication of being life-giving, to live in the present moment … It is vital because when we become aware and awake to the present moment, we are also awake to God, and then everything can become a moment of miracle, a mysterious reality.'[139]

Jesus invites us to become again like little children – to live in the present moment, to experience awe and wonder in what we see around us, to pause from the business and clutter of our daily lives.

Resting

I think that may be one reason why the Sabbath is such an important concept in the Bible. God wants us to take time to rest,

---

[139] E. de Waal. *Lost in wonder.* Norwich, UK: Canterbury Press, 2003, 59.

to enjoy his creation. The very origin of the Sabbath lies in rest: 'By the seventh day God had finished the work he had been doing; so on the seventh day he rested from all his work. And God blessed the seventh day and made it holy, because on it he rested from all the work of creating that he had done.'[140] This rest follows directly on from God completing his creation, seeing all he had made, and enjoying it as 'very good'. Perhaps God too had a childlike expression of awe and wonder at what he saw.

And so God gave us a command to rest, perhaps realising that we don't do this well. We rest so we can pause in our work and appreciate the beauty of God's creation.

Again, I think this is something children do much better than adults. Children love to rest and play. In doing so, they are expressing who they are, their very nature as children created by God, in God's image and in relation to other people and to the world around them.

Caring for creation

The Sabbath principle also seems to reflect something of caring for creation. Both Sabbath and its extension in Jubilee were set as systems for restoration. The Sabbath year[141] and the Jubilee year[142] were established to allow the land itself to rest and recover, and for equity and justice to rule. In the Jubilee year, all land was to be returned to its original owners, people were to be set free:

> Consecrate the fiftieth year and proclaim liberty throughout the land to all its inhabitants. It shall be a jubilee for you; each one of you is to return to his family property and each to his own clan. The fiftieth year shall be a jubilee for you; do not sow and do not reap what grows of itself or harvest the

---

[140] Genesis 2:2–3.
[141] Leviticus 25:4.
[142] Leviticus 25:10.

untended vines. For it is a jubilee and is to be holy for you.[143]

So our growing awareness of creation involves a growing sense of responsibility to creation. We need to capture the Sabbath principle of caring for creation. It is part of our central being that we were created to care for and tend creation: 'The Lord God took the man and put him in the Garden of Eden to work it and take care of it.'[144] In doing so, we will find rest and beauty, and that in turn will lead us into praise of the God who made it all.

Awareness of God

Those early questions of 'Who am I?' 'Where did I come from?' and 'Who made me?' reveal a deeper search for identity and meaning. We seem to instinctively feel that there must be something more to life than that which is immediately apparent. We all probably, at some times, experience an inner restlessness that can make us very unsettled. St Augustine expressed it very powerfully: 'Thou madest us for Thyself, and our heart is restless, until it repose in Thee.'[145]

This sense of unrest or disquiet often seems to come to a head during adolescence. I think this period between childhood and adulthood is actually quite a crucial stage in our spiritual development. The concrete certainties with which the child was able to live gradually get shaken, and in their place comes a growing search for something that will give meaning to life. There also comes a growing frustration that nothing seems to be able to do so. In the

---

[143] Leviticus 25:10–12.

[144] Genesis 2:15.

[145] *Confessions of St Augustine*, Book 1, Chapter 1. www.online-literature.com/saint-augustine/confessions-of-saint-augustine/1/ Accessed 20.5.14

words of the Teacher in Ecclesiastes: 'Meaningless! Meaningless! ...
Utterly meaningless! Everything is meaningless.'[146]

The book of Ecclesiastes is an intriguing book that tends to
puzzle people: why include in the Bible a book which is so full of
uncertainties, that seems to go round in circles, filled with existential
teenage angst? I think that the answer may lie in this whole area
of spiritual development, and that this may be one of the most
important books of the Bible. The Teacher, with all his questioning
and experiences, seems to mirror what many of us go through in our
search for God. He starts his journey very clearly with that sense that
everything is meaningless:

> What does man gain from all his labour
> at which he toils under the sun?
> Generations come and generations go,
> but the earth remains for ever ...
> What has been will be again,
> what has been done will be done again;
> there is nothing new under the sun.[147]

From that starting point, the Teacher sets out on a journey
to discover meaning. He searches for wisdom through study and
learning, and concludes, 'This, too, is a chasing after the wind. For
with much wisdom comes much sorrow; the more knowledge, the
more grief.'[148]

He then turns to pleasure, laughter, and wine, but these also
prove to be meaningless: '"Laughter," I said, "is foolish. And what
does pleasure accomplish?"'[149]

Next, he works hard to accumulate wealth and property and all
that go with it:

---

[146] Ecclesiastes 1:2.

[147] Ecclesiastes 1:3–9.

[148] Ecclesiastes 1:17–18.

[149] Ecclesiastes 2:1–2.

I denied myself nothing my eyes desired; I refused my heart no pleasure. My heart took delight in all my work, and this was the reward for all my labour. Yet when I surveyed all that my hands had done and what I had toiled to achieve, everything was meaningless, a chasing after the wind; nothing was gained under the sun.[150]

And so it goes on. The Teacher considers wisdom, status, riches, hard work, and ambition – and concludes that all that is meaningless. He also sees injustice, oppression, envy, greed, suffering, loneliness, and death, and finds no meaning in any of that. He even seems to suggest that both religion and philosophy are meaningless, and that righteous living is of no benefit.[151]

Idolatry

All this seems to mirror much of the behaviour displayed by teenagers. You, my dear daughter, will have seen it in your friends and others you came across, at school and university, and out and about. Young people search for meaning and pleasure through relationships, sex, possessions, partying, alcohol, and drugs. Others search through ambition, skills, sports, music, and exam results. Still others try to find it in religious experience of all kinds. But in the end, none of this can ever fully fill that emptiness. That is surely because this void can only be filled by the God who created us and who put that longing in our hearts.

I suspect this may be why the Bible is so strong in condemning idolatry. The first two of the Ten Commandments are about idolatry – commanding the Israelites to have no other gods before God, and not to make or bow down before any idol.[152] Similarly the

---

[150]   Ecclesiastes 2: 10–11.

[151]   Ecclesiastes 5: 1–3, 7; 7:15; 8:17; 9:2; 12:12.

[152]   Exodus 20:3–4.

prophets frequently speak out against it, as do Paul, John, and Peter in their letters.[153]

We may not bow down to physical idols, but, as Paul makes clear in his letters, immorality and greed are forms of idolatry.[154] Anything we seek in place of God, whether through religion, relationships, ambition, or greed, displaces God from God's rightful place. God knows that ultimately none of these things can satisfy us. He wants to protect us from the hopelessness and despair that will ultimately come if we try to fill the gap with these.

Finding God

There is hope though because God also wants to be found by us, and he provides the way through which we can do so. God promises that we can find him:

> [If] you seek the Lord your God, you will find him
> if you look for him with all your heart and with all
> your soul.[155]

> You will seek me and find me when you seek me
> with all your heart. I will be found by you.[156]

Jesus also emphasises this in his Sermon on the Mount: 'Ask and it will be given to you; seek and you will find; knock and the door will be opened to you. For everyone who asks receives; he who seeks finds; and to him who knocks the door will be opened.'[157] Surprisingly, Isaiah even goes so far as to suggest that God can be

---

[153] See, for example, Isaiah 44: 9; Habakkuk 2:18; Galatians 5:19–21; 1 Peter 4:3; 1 John 5:21.
[154] Ephesians 5:5; Colossians 3:5.
[155] Deuteronomy 4:29.
[156] Jeremiah 29:13–14.
[157] Matthew 7:7–8.

found by those who are not seeking: 'I revealed myself to those who did not ask for me; I was found by those who did not seek me.'[158]

So, if God wants to be found by us, and if we are restless until we find him; if, as the Teacher suggests, all of our attempts to find fulfilment and meaning lead to nothing, how do we connect to the Divine?

One of the most staggering aspects of the Bible's teaching on this is that it seems that God cannot be found through religion, not even through Christianity as a religion. Indeed, if anything, God seems to frown on religion:

> I hate, I despise your religious feasts; I cannot stand your assemblies. Even though you bring me burnt offerings and grain offerings, I will not accept them. Though you bring choice fellowship offerings, I will have no regard for them. Away with the noise of your songs! I will not listen to the music of your harps.[159]

Isaiah echoes this sentiment:

> Day after day they seek me out; they seem eager to know my ways, as if they were a nation that does what is right and has not forsaken the commands of its God. They ask me for just decisions and seem eager for God to come near them. 'Why have we fasted,' they say, 'and you have not seen it? Why have we humbled ourselves and you have not noticed?'[160]

Jesus, too, is highly critical of the religious leaders of his day, suggesting that rather than helping others to find God, they are actually keeping people from him:

---

[158]   Isaiah 65:1.
[159]   Amos 5:21–23.
[160]   Isaiah 58:2–3.

> Woe to you, teachers of the law and Pharisees, you
> hypocrites! You shut the kingdom of heaven in
> men's faces. You yourselves do not enter, nor will
> you let those enter who are trying to.[161]

A lot of this criticism of religion is linked to hypocrisy
(interestingly, something that young people are very quick to spot
and to condemn) and particularly to injustice. Nevertheless, it seems
clear to me that religion, in itself, cannot bring us to God.

Finding God in Jesus

As I understand it, the key message of the Gospel is that God is
not found through any kind of human endeavour, but simply and
exclusively in a person – Jesus. That is why Jesus seems to make
such outrageous claims about himself: 'I am the way, the truth and
the life. No one comes to the Father except through me.'[162] 'I am
the resurrection and the life. He who believes in me will live, even
though he die.'[163]

Through Jesus we can come to know God, and in place of the
restlessness that marks our spiritual development, we can find peace
and a full, abundant life which has meaning and purpose. Jesus
himself said, 'I have come that [you] might have life, and have it to
the full.'[164] He promises to give us rest: 'Come to me, all you who
are weary and burdened, and I will give you rest.'[165]

The account of little children being brought to Jesus is one of
my favourite passages in the Bible:

---

[161]   Matthew 23:13.

[162]   John 14:6.

[163]   John 11:25.

[164]   John 10:10.

[165]   Matthew 11:28.

> People were bringing little children to Jesus to have him touch them, but the disciples rebuked them. When Jesus saw this, he was indignant. He said to them, 'Let the little children come to me, and do not hinder them, for the kingdom of God belongs to such as these. I tell you the truth, anyone who will not receive the kingdom of God like a little child will never enter it.' And he took the children in his arms, put his hands on them and blessed them.[166]

Jesus was indignant at his disciples trying to prevent the children coming to him. And when these children did come to him, he didn't try to teach them or give them lots of instructions. He simply took them in his arms and blessed them.

I think that was his way of demonstrating that coming to God is not something complex or something that requires us to do the right things or ask the right questions. It is simply a question of starting a relationship with Jesus. I think when Jesus says the kingdom of God belongs to children, he is inviting us to go backwards, to a stage before all our adolescent yearnings, and start a relationship in the simple, trusting way that a young child will start a relationship.

Setting Foundations

Although I believe this adolescent questioning and journey of discovery is an essential part of our spiritual development, I do not think it inevitably leads to damaging behaviours and a sense of hopelessness.

I was privileged to grow up in a loving home with parents who cared for me, modelled a life of loving service, and gave me

---

[166]   Mark 10:13–16.

foundations from which to navigate through this turbulent time of seeking God. Ultimately, I had to discover God for myself, but I think I was spared much of the trauma that so many people face, and I was spared because of these foundations.

Dearest Esther, it has been such a blessing to me to see how you too have grown into a young adult and come to discover God yourself. I am frequently grateful to God for the way you and your brother have developed, and grateful too for all that your mother gave you as you were growing.

Part of this came from setting moral foundations, laying down rules and discipline at an early stage. You learned to distinguish right from wrong and, in time, to make wise choices based on that. This is what is suggested in Proverbs: 'Train a child in the way he should go, and when he is old he will not turn from it.'[167] It is why such emphasis was placed on the Israelites teaching God's laws to their children:

> Fix these words of mine in your hearts and minds;
> tie them as symbols on your hands and bind them
> on your foreheads. Teach them to your children,
> talking about them when you sit at home and when
> you walk along the road, when you lie down and
> when you get up.[168]

It is interesting that this teaching is a whole-life experience. The Deuteronomy passage suggests a constant weaving of God's laws into every part of life; something that would involve talking about God and modelling this lifestyle throughout the day, not simply learning about it on the Sabbath.

Setting the foundations for a child to discover God, however, involves far more than teaching or modelling a moral code. It is

---

[167] Proverbs 22:6.
[168] Deuteronomy 11:18–19.

something that is rooted in relationship. Perhaps the greatest gifts a parent can give his child are to introduce her to Jesus, show her how she can have a living, meaningful relationship with him, and demonstrate, through parenting, the loving nature of God the Father.

Discovering God's character

It is one of the most awful[169] responsibilities of being a parent that a child's perception of God will be influenced most by what she sees of the Holy One in her parents. If we talk of God as Father, a child will interpret that in the light of what she perceives her father to be.

If a child experiences her parents as non-attentive, absent, or not interested in her, it is likely that she will form an image of God as absent and not interested. If she experiences her parents as authoritarian, rigid, and harsh in their discipline, that is how she will perceive God. If she experiences her parents as unpredictable or violent, she very easily transfers that experience to her perception of God.

If, however, her parents show her unconditional love, valuing her for who she is, believing in her, encouraging her, helping her to grow, supporting her when she is upset or frightened, forgiving her when she has done wrong, and always being there to welcome her and shower her with affection, that will help her form a true image of God as her loving, caring Father. If the child grows up with such an understanding of who God is and what God is like, she will find it far easier to turn to God when she goes through this journey of discovery.

---

[169] I use this term in the deep sense of inspiring 'reverential wonder or fear' (*Chambers English Dictionary*. Cambridge: Chambers, 1988, 97.)

From a point of a healthy relationship with God as a loving, heavenly Father, I believe a child is able to grow in her awareness of other aspects of God's character.

If her starting point is an awareness of God as loving and forgiving, she can appreciate the Holy One as powerful – omnipotent, omniscient, and omnipresent – and respond in worship rather than fear. Instead of seeing God as a distant, absent architect, she can marvel at creation, enjoying the beauty and majesty of all that the Creator is making, delighting in it as a young child. Instead of being cowed by images of God as a terrible judge, she can see God's holiness and justice as out-workings of grace in response to the cries of the oppressed, setting limits on evil and suffering.

All this can lead to a right attitude of worship, adoration, and praise. As that right awareness of God grows in her, she will find the fulfilment of her true identity and can join the hymn of all creation, singing,

> To him who sits on the throne and to the Lamb
> Be praise and honour and glory and power,
> For ever and ever![170]

---

[170] Revelation 5:13.

9

IMAGE

God created mankind in his own image, in the image of
God he created them; male and female he created them.

- Genesis 1:27

My dear Esther, over the past few chapters we have explored how children develop in strength, mind, heart, and soul. We have seen how these aspects of child development give us insights into what it means to become like a little child. This whole process is fascinating and a delight to watch. As you have grown to adulthood, I have loved watching these processes unfold in your life.

Equally fascinating, though, is the question of why children develop along these lines. What is it that drives a child's development? Reflecting on this, I think that an understanding of what drives development gives us some important insights into what it means to be created in God's image. It is that question that I want to explore in this chapter.

From a purely biological and evolutionary standpoint, the primary, if not the only, driver of development must be a drive towards independence: to ensure that the child survives and grows to reproductive maturity so as to propagate the human species and to perpetuate his or her genes.

That is obviously an important factor, and we can see how it influences a lot of what we see in a child's development. The physical growth and development of the human body enables us to reach a stage of sexual maturity so as to be able to reproduce. The development of an upright stance and the ability to manipulate objects with our hands facilitates our ability to obtain food and ensure warmth and security. One could argue that this gives us an evolutionary advantage over other animals. The development of language and other skills of social interaction promotes our ability to find a mate.

That is all very good as far as it goes, but it seems to me to be very limited in explaining the complexity and intricacies of all aspects of human development that we have been exploring above. While survival remains a vitally important factor in driving a child's development, there are three other key drivers or motivators that seem to me to be equally prominent: creativity, relationship, and exploration. These three characteristics help to explain why a child develops the way she does, and I think show us something about what it means to be created in God's image. We can add them to our model of child development.

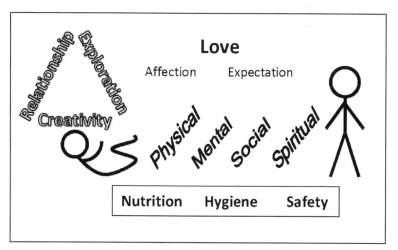

A model of child development

Creativity

Children are creative. We see this expressed in lots of ways from a very early stage. If you give a young child a box of bricks, she will build a tower or a bridge or a train. If you give her a crayon, she will draw a picture. If you give her a puzzle, she will try to put it together. This creativity is one of the primary drivers of her fine motor development. It certainly helps to explain why our manipulative skills do not stop at the point of being able to grasp and release.

As we have seen, over the first year, infants lose their primitive grasp reflex and learn to voluntarily grasp and then release objects. These basic fine motor skills are important, allowing the child to obtain food and feed herself. But there is a further development that goes beyond the very basic grasp and release functions.

To start with, the child grabs objects with a whole-hand palmar grasp. All her fingers and her thumb enclose and hold an object, and all of them let go when she releases. She then slowly moves to a 'scissor grip', holding objects between her thumb and fingers, using the whole length of her digits. This, in turn, is gradually refined as a more and more specific 'pincer grip'.

At the same time, her ability to locate objects becomes gradually more refined, moving from a general 'raking' in the vague direction of the object she desires to a much more directed movement towards the object's location. This refinement allows the child to pick up and manipulate increasingly small objects. This happens much to the horror of her anxious parents, as some of these small objects find their way into her mouth, nose, ears, and elsewhere.

Building

Manipulative refinement also allows a child to do more and more complex and creative tasks. Building things, whether from simple wooden bricks, Lego, Meccano, or other materials, requires finesse in using her fingers; it also requires the child to coordinate her hands and her vision, and to use both hands together.

Up to about the age of 2 or 3, a young child will place bricks on top of each other, one at a time, using one hand only. There is a limit to how high she can build her tower this way. Much more than about six bricks and the tower will start to lean and eventually fall. Later, though, she learns to use one hand to stabilise her tower while the other builds above it, enabling her to reach ever higher in her attempts to produce inspiring creations.

Drawing

Another area in which we see the child's motor development being driven by creativity is in her drawing. If you give an infant a crayon, she will probably put it in her mouth and chew it (part of her exploration of the world). However, she quickly learns that these amazing waxy objects make marks when you push them across a paper or a desk or a wall. So she starts to draw.

At first this will just be random marks on the paper. Then she starts to scribble – first in a to-and-fro manner, then in a circular form. Then, as her manipulative skills improve, she learns to stop as well as start and to position her crayon on the paper. She learns to draw horizontal and vertical lines, then circles, triangles, squares, and diamonds, and then increasingly complex shapes and pictures.

Interestingly, a child's first recognisable pictures are almost invariably pictures of people. I think this says a lot about what is important to the young child. The nature of these people-pictures also tells us a lot about how the young child perceives her world and the people in it. The very earliest people-pictures tend to consist of a head, with eyes and a smiling mouth, and two long legs. Legs and faces: that is primarily what children see of the adult world they inhabit. But this is important, and the faces, in particular, emphasise the importance to the child of positive interaction and loving relationships.

Play

Creativity isn't limited to building and drawing or other fine-motor aspects of development. We also see creativity shining through children's play, their communication, and the way they use their minds.

Children love to play. That is perhaps one of the most striking aspects of childhood. Interestingly, their play largely seems to revolve around a combination of creativity, exploration, and relationship. If you give a child a box of bricks or a crayon, she will create something with them. If you leave a group of children in a garden, it probably won't be long before they start playing hide-and-seek. And if you watch children singing nursery rhymes, you will see beautiful examples of relationship – even in the very simple act of joining hands in a circle, dancing round and round, and all falling down.

A lot of children's play revolves around the use of their imaginations. And this too is creative. When you were still very young, Esther, you acquired a doll, whom you named Ah-Lee. Ah-Lee quickly became your constant companion, travelling with you wherever you went. Your play with Ah-Lee showed your ability to create a world for Ah-Lee, with you as her loving parent. In another, delightful stage of your development, when you were three, you had an imaginary alter-ego called Bedi, who had a naughty friend, Bullat. Bullat seemed to be responsible for most of your wrongdoing – a very useful deflection!

As you got older, the imaginary games became more and more complex, often with elaborate plots drawing on your experience of the world and whatever books or films were popular at the time. Typical themes when you were at primary school were mixtures of Narnia, Star Wars, and the Redwall books, with you playing the part of Queen Amidala or Princess Leia or the squirrel maids from Redwall.

Your creativity also came through as you learned to speak – first playing with different sounds, enjoying their rhythms and tones, then forming them into recognisable words and sentences. You loved making animal sounds when you were very young: 'rar', 'grr', 'sss', and your favourite 'mao-mao' for a cat.

You expressed your creativity through singing too – nursery rhymes, then songs. All kinds of music, from banging a wooden spoon on a saucepan right through to your more recent Beethoven sonatas and other piano pieces, were expressions of your creativity. These brought immense joy both to you as the musician and to us as your audience.

A creative God

If we think of ourselves as made in the image of God, this aspect of children's development is easy to relate to what we know about God – God is a creative God. In the beginning, God spoke, and all things came into being. God created the heavens and the earth. The Bible highlights this creativity – most notably in the beautiful parallels between the creation story in Genesis and the New Testament accounts of Jesus's role in creation.

> In the beginning God created the heavens and the earth.[171]

> In the beginning was the Word,
> and the Word was with God,
> and the Word was God.
> He was with God in the beginning.
> Through him all things were made;
> without him nothing was made that has been made.[172]

---

[171] Genesis 1:1.
[172] John 1:1–3.

> He is the image of the invisible God,
> the firstborn over all creation.
> For by him all things were created:
> things in heaven and on earth, visible and invisible,
> whether thrones or powers or rulers or authorities;
> all things were created by him and for him.[173]

If we see God as the Creator and Jesus, the image of the invisible God, also creating, then it is not surprising that we, who also are made in the image of God, should be creative.

As adults, most of us are very achievement and purpose focused. When we create things, we often do so as a means to an end, rather than as an end in itself. But if we watch children in their creative play, I think we see creation as an end in itself. The very act of creating is something pleasurable and meaningful.

Our creativity expresses something of our own nature and also something of the nature of God, our Creator. Your music and the kinds of things you like to play, Esther, reflect something of your personality. So too did all your creativity as you were growing.

Above our mantelpiece we have hung a wonderful piece of artwork that you produced while at school. This collage presents a piano and a flute in contrasting tones. I love this piece of art, as it expresses something of who you are – the way you see things and what inspires you.

So it is with God. His creation expresses something of his nature and who he is:

> The heavens declare the glory of God;
> the skies proclaim the work of his hands.
> Day after day they pour forth speech;
> night after night they display knowledge.

---

[173] Colossians 1:15–16.

There is no speech or language where their voice is
not heard.
Their voice goes out into all the earth,
their words to the ends of the world.[174]

I think one aspect of Jesus's call to us to become like little children is to rediscover our creativity. Whether through art, music, writing, dance, gardening, juggling, or any other creative form, we need to discover and nurture our creative gifts. We need to do so not to achieve a purpose, but simply for the sake of being creative, of expressing who we are, and for the very pleasure of creating.

So as you continue through the adult world of work, responsibility, and purpose-driven life, my precious daughter, don't lose touch with your creative self. Whatever form that takes, give it space and enjoy your creative play – that is a large part of who God created you to be.

Relationship

Social development is one of the four aspects of our humanness that we explored earlier in this book. As they grow, children learn to develop social relationships, to communicate, and to interact with others. These developing social relationships are not only one of the core components of child development; they are also, I believe, one of the key factors that drives a child's development. The desire to relate is intensely strong and promotes responses in the child that lead to the development of skills in all areas of her development.

Initially, this is linked to survival, as the child interacts with her mother. But it seems to me that this interaction, the attachment behaviour we have considered above, goes beyond survival to a much deeper bond. There is a very strong element of affection between the

---

174   Psalm 19:1–6.

child and her mother. This affection persists even when the child has gained independence and has separated from her family home.

As you grew up, Esther, your social world gradually expanded. To start with, it consisted primarily of your mum and me. Interaction with others was almost entirely through the two of us and was regulated by us. But other people came into that world – your grandparents, other members of our family and close friends, and other babies who had been born around the same time.

In the second half of your first year, though, as you became more strongly attached to the two of us, you became very wary of others. Anyone you didn't know was initially treated with suspicion until given approval by one of us, and until that person earned your acceptance by proving to be friendly and non-threatening.

This wariness is an important survival mechanism, and we see it consistently in all babies. As they start to explore their world and gradually move away from the security of their mothers' proximity, infants become more vulnerable and so need to develop defences. However, they come through this.

Community

My dear Esther, as I reflect on your early years, I recall that it didn't take you long to overcome your fears and become a very sociable little girl. Just before your first birthday, we moved to Cambodia, and you quickly made friends with the other adults who were with us on the team. Then your social circle started to take on its own identity – through other children you met in our street, through church, through toddler groups, and so on. Back in England, your social world spread out like ripples on a pond to encompass friends from playgroup, then school and other activities.

This broadening community is an important part of what it means to be a human. It helped to drive your development in all sorts of ways – in your language, your play, your physical activity, your thinking. It also helped to shape your character: who you are and what makes you tick. I think your early experiences in Cambodia, moving house frequently in your first four years, and being introduced very rapidly to a wide range of different people have contributed to your very outgoing and easy nature.

When we first came back from Cambodia, one of your favourite activities was to take me by the hand and go and sit on the pavement outside the front of our house. It puzzled you that the road was so quiet, without loads of people wandering around or stopping to talk with us, but it was still fun just to sit and watch the world. Just sitting beside me, your father, was, in itself, a social activity, spurred on by a longing for relationship. Those moments of sitting with you remain with me as a treasured memory.

Intimacy

Hand in hand with this broadening of the child's social world goes a persistent intimacy with those closest to her. While you were able to make lots of friends as you went to school, you remained very close to your mum and me, and to your brother Joseph. Within your wide circle of friends, there were just a few with whom you remained very close.

Those close relationships are incredibly important. It is the intimate friends who most help shape who we are and the way we behave. In any child's development, as she goes through school years and into adolescence, her peer relationships are incredibly important.

Sadly, this can easily go wrong if a child gets in with the wrong crowd and succumbs to the pressures to rebel or to conform in unhelpful ways, such as through smoking, alcohol, drugs, or sexual experiences.

The exhortation of Psalm 1 is so true: 'Blessed is the man who does not walk in the counsel of the wicked or stand in the way of sinners or sit in the seat of mockers.'[175] The book of Proverbs is

---

[175] Psalm 1:1.

full of advice about friendships and our wider relationships, and similarly emphasises the importance of this intimacy: 'A man of many companions may come to ruin, but there is a friend who sticks closer than a brother.'[176]

A relational God

These twin aspects of relationship – community and intimacy – reflect a further aspect of what it means to be made in the image of God. We see something of this in Andrei Rublev's famous icon of the Trinity, which depicts the three angels who visited Abraham near Mamre.[177] The icon also captures something of the mystery of the Trinity. In it we see the three angels, or the representations of the Father, Son, and Holy Spirit, sitting together at a table, in intimate communion.

The very concept of God as one God in three persons captures the essence of this relationship – at the very heart, God is a god of intimate relationship. We see this intimacy in God's affirmation of Jesus at his baptism and transfiguration: 'This is my son, whom I love; with him I am well pleased.'[178] We see it also in Jesus' clear statement that 'I and the Father are one.'[179]

The most wonderful thing about this intimate relationship, though, is that it is not exclusive. In Rublev's icon there is space for another at the table. Within the heart of God there is space for us to enter into that same intimacy. God's relational nature spreads beyond the intimacy of the Trinity to welcome all into a loving community. But it goes even further in that, unlike us, God is able to extend intimacy to every single person who comes into that community, and he wants all people everywhere to do so.

---

[176] Proverbs 18:24.
[177] Genesis 18:1–15.
[178] Matthew 3:17; 17:5.
[179] John 10:30.

> Therefore, if anyone is in Christ, that person
> is a new creation: The old has gone, the new is
> here! All this is from God, who reconciled us to
> himself through Christ and gave us the ministry
> of reconciliation: that God was reconciling the
> world to himself in Christ, not counting people's
> sins against them. And he has committed to us the
> message of reconciliation.[180]

Jesus specifically invited his disciples to share in the intimate relationship he had with his Father: 'On that day you will realize that I am in my Father, and you are in me, and I am in you.'[181] Jesus prayed for his disciples and for all, including you and me, who believe in him, 'That all of them may be one, Father, just as you are in me and I am in you. May they also be in us so that the world may believe that you have sent me.'[182]

Sexual intimacy

In some wonderful but mysterious way which I don't really understand, this intimate relationship within God's nature is reflected in the deep intimacy of a sexual relationship, and particularly in the union between a man and a woman in marriage.

Discovering your sexual identity and learning to ultimately express that in the security and faithfulness of a marriage relationship is one of the most important, wonderful, and at the same time painful aspects of growing up. Again it is an area in which so often children and young people can make mistakes.

Intimate relationships have the potential to cause immense pain. The more intimate the relationship, the more painful any separation or disagreement. Conversely, though, this intimacy brings

---

[180] 2 Corinthians 5:17–19.

[181] John 14:20.

[182] John 17:21.

the potential for the most intense joy and warmth. I am so grateful for the wonderful intimacy I had with your mum, and for God's protection on our marriage, which allowed that intimacy to continue and grow.

This kind of intimate relationship is so close to the heart of God that Paul likens it to the relationship between Christ and the church:

> Husbands, love your wives, just as Christ loved the church and gave himself up for her to make her holy, cleansing her by the washing with water through the word, and to present her to himself as a radiant church, without stain or wrinkle or any other blemish, but holy and blameless. In this same way, husbands ought to love their wives as their own bodies. He who loves his wife loves himself. After all, no one ever hated their own body, but they feed and care for their body, just as Christ does the church – for we are members of his body. 'For this reason a man will leave his father and mother and be united to his wife, and the two will become one flesh.' This is a profound mystery – but I am talking about Christ and the church.[183]

Exploration

We have already seen how a relationship of love provides the secure base that babies need to start exploring their world. This exploration is one of the key drivers of development. It is a child's inquisitiveness that leads her to raise her head to look around, then lift up on her arms when prone, and subsequently get herself into a sitting, then standing position, both of which enable her to see more

---

[183]   Ephesians 5:25–32.

of the world. They also free up her hands to explore things through manipulation (and free them up for creativity).

Crawling, rolling, cruising, and walking are all guided by a desire to get around and explore her world. As time goes on, the young child goes further and further in her exploration. This promotes increasing independence as well as greater motor skills, such as running and climbing.

Babies use pretty well all of their bodies to explore their world. Their eyes and ears are fairly obvious means of seeing and hearing what is going on around them, and their hands are a primary means of touching and feeling. Babies love different textures – toys that feel different or that do things when manipulated. They also tend to use their mouths as primary organs of exploration. So, from the age of around six months, a baby will tend to put most objects up to her mouth as she works out the taste and texture of things. This tendency can be much to her parents' concern, especially when the object being put into her mouth is a tiny choking hazard, a handful of mud, or something even worse.

As she grows, a child will extend her exploration through her mind and her cognitive development; hence the importance of all those early questions. As we have already seen, these questions go gradually deeper as she seeks to understand the nature and meaning of her world. Ultimately I think this need to explore is related very strongly to a child's spiritual development and a drive to understand and know God, to discover her own identity, and to understand her place in the world and how she relates to other people.

This sense of exploration or inquisitiveness extends to a child's social relationships. She seeks out people with whom to form relationships. As she does so, she also seeks to know more about the person with whom she is relating.

Seeking

One of the first games children play is hide-and-seek and its various manifestations. The most basic form of hide-and-seek is probably peekaboo, a game you used to love. I remember clearly, my treasure, how you would squeal with delight when I or your mother would appear round a corner and say boo. You learned to take the initiative with peekaboo, but to start with you used to put your hands over your ears and your eyes to hide – thinking that if you couldn't hear or see us, we couldn't hear or see you. I think these games are an early means of the child learning to seek relationships with others in a safe environment with someone she knows. Through hiding, seeking, and finding, she is in effect repeatedly forming new relationships in a safe manner.

Hide-and-seek is perhaps the earliest recorded game in history, with its roots in the garden of Eden:

> Then the man and his wife heard the sound of the Lord God as he was walking in the garden in the cool of the day, and they hid from the Lord God among the trees of the garden. But the Lord God called to the man, 'Where are you?'[184]

A seeking God

Interestingly, it is God who is doing the seeking here. Perhaps, then, this developmental root of exploration can tell us not just about our own need to explore and discover, but also something about the nature of God himself.

If we are made in God's image, and our need to explore is a core part of our nature, this also says something about God's nature. While I don't think that God, being all knowing, needs to explore in

---

[184] Genesis 3:8–9.

the wider sense of discovering the world, I think we do see in the Bible a sense of God as a seeking God – seeking out people with whom he can form or reform relationships. This comes across strongly in the parable of the lost sheep, where Jesus likens God to a shepherd who goes out of his way to seek one sheep who has gone missing.[185]

So in a sense this seeking is a two-way process: our whole beings are created to explore, and ultimately this deep-seated drive leads us to seek for God, without whom we will always be incomplete. At the same time, God is seeking us, longing to be reconciled with us. And so, as we saw in the last chapter, we can have confidence that we will find him: "'You will seek me and find me when you seek me with all your heart. I will be found by you,' declares the Lord.'[186]

I will be found by you

---

[185]   Luke 15:3–7.

[186]   Jeremiah 29:13–14.

These three characteristics – creativity, relationship, and exploration –reflect something of the nature of God. They emphasise some aspects of what it means for us to be created in God's image and what motivates us to develop into that image. As such, they capture a part of what it means to be born again and become like a little child. In doing so we need to rediscover what it means to be creative, to explore, to discover, and to form relationships in community and intimacy.

These characteristics mirror the four aspects of spiritual development that we discussed in the last chapter: awareness of ourselves, awareness of God, awareness of creation, and awareness of others. Discovering our creativity in whatever form that takes is an important part of finding our identity, made in God's image to reflect God's character. Our inherent inquisitiveness leads us to explore and discover the world, and ultimately leads us to seek God, the Creator of our world. And our yearning for relationship drives us to relate to others around us and, with them and all creation through Jesus, to be brought into the most secure, intimate, loving relationship of all, with God:

'For God was pleased to have all his fullness dwell in [Jesus], and through him to reconcile to himself all things, whether things on earth or things in heaven, by making peace through his blood, shed on the cross.'[187]

---

[187] Colossians 1:19–20.

10

INHERITANCE

Now if we are children, then we are heirs –
heirs of God and co-heirs with Christ.

- Romans 8:17

The common interpretation of the word 'inheritance' is 'what you get from your parents when they die'. My dear daughter, I'm afraid by that token you and your brother are on to a bit of a loser. Several generations ago, the Sidebotham family were fairly wealthy landowners in Manchester, with a number of thriving family businesses profiting from the industrial revolution. All that wealth has long since gone.

I'm sorry, but for you there will be no fine mansion, no grand title or famous name to parade to, not even a string of priceless pearls to grace your beautiful neck. The best you can hope for are some rather battered pieces of furniture, half a library of accumulated books, and a small collection of stamps to split between you and your brother.

But perhaps that is no bad thing. Possessions seem to have a knack of creating havoc in families, and only get in the way of a simple lifestyle. Besides which, you can't take them with you when you finally go. I hope, dear Esther, that perhaps we have given you something far more lasting and worthwhile.

In reality, an inheritance is far more than the material possessions left to you by your parents. What a child inherits from her parents is richer, deeper, and more profound than a sum of money. Who you are and what you become is a product of your inheritance: both the genes that are passed on to you, setting your potential, and the environment that you grow up in – your parents' attitudes and behaviour, your wider family, and your influences outside the family – all combine to mould you into what you finally become. This combination of nature and nurture is what forms you, from the moment of conception on. This, however, brings a dilemma, for while your genes are fixed, the nurture side of the equation isn't. And it can go either way, bringing both positive and negative inheritances.

The sin of the fathers

One of the most troubling statements in the whole Bible comes with the second of the ten commandments: 'I, the Lord your God, am a jealous God, punishing the children for the sin of the fathers to the third and fourth generation of those who hate me, but showing love to a thousand generations of those who love me and keep my commandments.'[188] This seems to fly in the face of all our assurances of God's unconditional love. The love of God expressed in these verses seems totally conditional – on being loved and obeyed. And, worse still, the converse seems to be a completely unjust punishment of the children for their fathers' sins.

In my work in child protection, I see all too clearly the reality of the first half of these verses, but in a way that suggests an alternative understanding. I find it very difficult to accept that a loving, gracious

---

[188]   Exodus 20:5–6.

God could inflict punishment on children for their fathers' sins, and I'm not sure that is what these verses are intended to convey. Perhaps it is more a statement of the consequences of sin. For, as troubling as it may be, all too often it is the children who suffer. Perhaps, rather than a statement of God's intent or of what he wants, it is more an observation of reality.

When parents (fathers or mothers) abuse or neglect their children, those children suffer pain. But the effects are even more profound, for the abuse or neglect inflicted on children stays with them as they grow, affecting their development.

When a child grows up without the nutrition, hygiene, or safety she needs, she will not thrive, and her development will be impaired. All aspects of physical, mental, social, and spiritual development are affected. And, as we have already seen, even with the provision of physical care and nurture, without the parental love that is so crucial, she won't thrive. The young child whose parent puts her down, threatens her, or fails to show affection will grow up believing she is unloved and unlovable.

We know that children who have been abused, particularly those who have been emotionally or sexually abused, can experience a whole host of long-term effects of that abuse, including educational failure, social exclusion, and behaviour difficulties, along with relationship difficulties, mental health problems, and addictive behaviour in adult life. I think a lot of these difficulties can be traced back to the child being robbed of three core values: faith, hope, and love.

A child whose parent is unpredictable, who hits out at her, who hurts her rather than loving her will not be able to trust the very person whom she most needs to trust. Slowly, she will lose the ability to trust, until eventually any faith or trust becomes an unattainable ideal.

A child who has no control over what happens to her, to whom things are done, who knows only pain and denigration will lose the ability to hope. She will come to believe that she cannot influence her future and will be unable to conceive that things could be different.

A child who does not receive a parent's love will feel herself unloved and unworthy. In time, she will believe that she is truly unlovable and that no one, not even God, could possibly love her.

Those influences carry on, even to the next generation. It is a very sad reality that there is an intergenerational cycle of abuse. A person who was abused in her childhood carries the effects of that abuse with her into her future relationships. Sadly, she is more vulnerable to others who will exploit and abuse her and her children. Those who grow up experiencing abuse have no normal model of parenting on which to base their own parenting. As a result they may go on to inflict harm on their own children, or fail to provide them with the love and nurture they need. This is the devastating reality of the 'sin of the fathers' being visited on their children to the third and fourth generation: the next generations do suffer as a consequence of the ongoing impact of the behaviours, attitudes, and values of their parents.

Looked at another way, however, these two verses in Exodus convey a very different reality, and one that displays something of God's amazing grace. The language of jealousy and punishment may not be easy, but if we interpret these verses in the context of observed reality, we see God setting limits on the extent of this intergenerational suffering.

In contrast to the 'thousand generations' experiencing his love, God actually sets a limit of just three to four generations experiencing the consequences of sin. And so there is hope. Even though intergenerational cycles of abuse are seen, they are not inevitable. Indeed, the majority of those who experience abuse in their childhood do not go on to abuse their children. People do break out and are set free. While children do undoubtedly suffer for their parents' sins, it is clearly not God's intent that this should go on indefinitely.

A protective jealousy

It is worth exploring the context of God's warning and promise in Exodus chapter 20. These are linked to the second commandment: 'You shall not make for yourself an idol in the form of anything in heaven above or on the earth beneath or in the waters below. You shall not bow down to them or worship them; for I, the Lord your God, am a jealous God.'[189] And through that, to the first commandment: 'You shall have no other gods before me.'[190]

God's 'jealousy' is, I believe, a protective jealousy. The Holy One set these laws to protect his children. That protection goes beyond protection from cruelty and the effects of abuse and violence. God wants to protect us also from the far more subtle effects of idolatry. Here too we see the reality of the sins of the fathers being visited on their children. For we do inherit the values and idolatry of our parents. This is far more subtle, but I suspect also more widespread and insidious, than the intergenerational cycle of violence and abuse that I have described above.

No matter how hard we may try not to, as parents we inevitably pass on some of our values to our children. If what we value is riches, a comfortable life with all we could need or wish for, that is what our children will inherit – along with the binding greed, the fear of loss, and the indifference to the needs of others that such idolatry brings with it. If what we value is achievement, status, and power, that is what our children will inherit – along with the low self-esteem, the constant striving to be good enough, the bullying, and the exploitation that come with that idolatry. If what we seek is pleasure and indulgence, an easy life, fun and action, and a wide circle of friends, we will pass that on to our children – along with the emptiness that so often sneaks in with this idolatry, the fear of pain, and the loneliness of absent love.

---

[189] Exodus 20:4–5.
[190] Exodus 20:3.

Of course, comfort, achievement, and pleasure are all good things. But they are gifts from God. When we cease to see them in that light, with gratitude in our hearts to the Giver of all good things, they begin to supplant God, becoming gods in themselves, to which we become enslaved in idolatry. That is when we pass these things on to our children, and to their children, and their children's children.

But when we keep all these in their right place, and worship God and God alone, giving thanks to him for all that he has made, loving God and keeping his commandments, then we see the blessings of his love extending to a thousand generations.

Llandudno

On 24 June 2011, I visited Llandudno in North Wales. I wasn't sure quite what to expect, or whether I would enjoy it, but I immediately warmed to the place. Nestled on a little isthmus between two rocky outcrops – Great Orme and Little Orme – the small resort has managed to retain an incredible amount of charm. Yes, it has its share of tacky gift shops, arcades, and tea rooms, but they do not dominate, and the town, with its broad, sweeping promenade and wide streets, carries still an air of Victorian grandeur.

I parked at the western end and spent a wonderful hour climbing to the top of Great Orme. First, I headed up through small, winding streets with old guest houses clinging to the hillside, then on through some hidden and rather neglected terraced gardens, to emerge by a copper mine near the summit. As I came down off the small hill, my path took me through a better-tended public garden where a small plaque echoed the song in my heart with the words of Psalm 104: 'O Lord, How manifold are thy works! In wisdom hast thou made them all; the earth is full of thy riches.'[191]

---

[191]   Psalm 104:24.

My dear Esther, you may be wondering what all this has to do with inheritance and becoming like a child, but for me, and therefore for you, this town carries a deep significance. One hundred and fifty years ago, your great-great-great-great-grandfather also walked the path I took up over Great Orme. The Sidebotham family, with their patriarch Joseph, used to stay there for their family holidays.

One inheritance which remains in our family is a bundle of old family diaries. I have been captivated by reading of the Sidebotham family's expeditions to this Victorian seaside resort, their accounts supplemented by some fine sketches of the Ormes.

For me, reflecting as I walked in their footsteps, tracing my inheritance through four or five generations captures something of the essence of Exodus 20:5–6.

The Sidebotham family were wealthy; they owned a mine and a cotton mill. They were influential, being involved in politics, local governance, and promotion of the sciences and the arts. But it is very clear, reading their diaries, that they loved God and sought to obey their Maker in all areas of their lives. They strove tirelessly for the welfare of their workers, building a church and a school, and, as far as I can tell, used their influence to seek the good of their community. They lived upright lives and celebrated the blessings God had given.

As I reflect on the intervening years, through my grandfather and father right through to our own family, and all the potential I see in you and Joseph, I can see how God has continued to bless our family through several generations.

A thousand generations

Those blessings may extend over more than the five or six generations since my ancestor Joseph and his family. Already I can see them extending through to the next generation. But that is still a far cry from the 'thousand generations' promised in Exodus.

Working on an average childbearing age of 25 years, a very simple calculation puts a thousand generations at around 25,000 years. Now, we are just 2,000 years from when Jesus walked the earth, and perhaps close to 4,000 years from when God made a covenant with Abraham. So the implication is that God's blessing will extend for a lot longer yet.

That, surely, was the whole tenor of God's promise to Abraham: 'I will make you into a great nation and I will bless you; I will make your name great, and you will be a blessing. I will bless those who bless you, and whoever curses you I will curse; and all peoples on earth will be blessed through you.'[192] That promise extended far beyond Abraham's immediate family, and even beyond the Jewish race, to reach out to all peoples on earth. We see the outworking of that through what Jesus came to be, and through his death and resurrection. So we can look forward in hope to the full reality of those blessings, not just for us, but for 'every nation, tribe, language and people.'[193]

A similar sense comes across in Psalm 103, in which the psalmist reflects on our transience: 'As for man, his days are like grass, he flourishes like a flower of the field; the wind blows over it and it is gone, and its place remembers it no more.'[194] In contrast to that, the psalmist sets out God's everlasting love: 'But from everlasting to everlasting the Lord's love is with those who fear him, and his righteousness with their children's children – with those who keep his covenant and remember to obey his precepts.'[195]

So God's faithfulness and love never fail and never will fail. It is that faithfulness and love that God wants us to inherit. As we become like little children, we are born again into that wonderful inheritance. Finally set free from the tarnished inheritance we have

---

[192] Genesis 12:2–3.

[193] Revelation 7:9; 14:6.

[194] Psalm 103:15–16.

[195] Psalm 103:17–18.

received from our parents – for even when that inheritance is one of blessing and goodness, it can never be perfect and will always have elements of the false values of our culture and the world around us – we instead come into a shared inheritance, with Jesus, of his kingdom:

> Praise be to the God and Father of our Lord Jesus Christ! In his great mercy he has given us new birth into a living hope through the resurrection of Jesus Christ from the dead, and into an inheritance that can never perish, spoil or fade – kept in heaven for you, who through faith are shielded by God's power until the coming of the salvation that is ready to be revealed in the last time.[196]

Inheriting God's kingdom

It is interesting that Jesus didn't say to Nicodemus, 'If you want to become a Christian, you must be born again,' or 'If you want to be saved, you must be born again.' What he actually said was, 'I tell you the truth, no-one can see the kingdom of God unless he is born again.'[197] Similarly, all of his statements about becoming like little children were made in the context of entering, receiving, or owning the kingdom of heaven.[198]

Jesus wants us to enter into, to be a part of, to inherit his kingdom. The way we do that is by becoming like little children. We put ourselves in a vulnerable place where God can start to remould us, to instil in us divine values and attitudes, so that we

---

[196] 1 Peter 1:3–5.
[197] John 3:3.
[198] Matthew 18:3; 19:14; Mark 10:15.

start to behave, perhaps quite naively, the way our Creator wants us to: with justice, compassion, and righteousness.

The other place where we find Jesus talking about inheriting his kingdom is in the parable of the sheep and goats. Here, he describes the Son of Man turning to the sheep whom he has placed on his right:

> Then the King will say to those on his right, 'Come, you who are blessed by my Father; take your inheritance, the kingdom prepared for you since the creation of the world. For I was hungry and you gave me something to eat, I was thirsty and you gave me something to drink, I was a stranger and you invited me in, I needed clothes and you clothed me, I was sick and you looked after me, I was in prison and you came to visit me.'
>
> Then the righteous will answer him, 'Lord, when did we see you hungry and feed you, or thirsty and give you something to drink? When did we see you a stranger and invite you in, or needing clothes and clothe you? When did we see you sick or in prison and go to visit you?'
>
> The King will reply, 'I tell you the truth, whatever you did for one of the least of these brothers of mine, you did for me.'[199]

This is not a picture of those who, adult-like, have somehow striven to do the right thing. Rather it is a picture of those who, transformed by God's spirit, have been born again, with a new outlook on life and new values. They have opened their eyes to Jesus's kingdom and all that it means. For them, 'doing the right thing' was something that came naturally – they were unaware even that they had done it.

---

[199] Matthew 25:34–40.

That is what we are being born into when we are born again: not some individual, selfish, personal salvation that has no impact on those around us, but the beginning of a transformation of character, developing in us the values of Jesus's kingdom.

The theologian Tom Wright expresses this well in his book *Virtue reborn*:

> We don't become Christians by struggling with great moral effort to make ourselves good enough for God, but by the work of the Holy Spirit, bringing us to a faith which looks away from our selves and trusts, instead, in what God has done for us in Jesus Christ. But that work of the Spirit is precisely the work of bringing someone to new birth. And, as that person is reborn, the life into which he or she is brought, like a newborn baby blinking and crying a moment after delivery, is the life in which new "strengths" of character need to be nurtured and developed.[200]

Adoption

The most amazing thing about this inheritance, Esther, is that we are being brought into a relationship with God. We have seen how it is an inheritance of God's blessing and goodness, and how it is an inheritance of God's purpose for us. First and foremost, though, it is an inheritance as daughters and sons.

By being born again, we are adopted as God's children. No longer do we have to view God as a distant divine being; we can relate to the Holy One as a child to her father.

---

[200]   T. Wright. *Virtue reborn*. London: SPCK Publishing, 2010, preface x.

> Because you are sons, God sent the Spirit of his Son into our hearts, the Spirit who calls out, 'Abba, Father.' So you are no longer a slave, but a son; and since you are a son, God has made you also an heir.[201]

> For you did not receive a spirit that makes you a slave again to fear, but you received the Spirit of sonship. And by him we cry, 'Abba, Father.' The Spirit himself testifies with our spirit that we are God's children. Now if we are children, then we are heirs – heirs of God and co-heirs with Christ, if indeed we share in his sufferings in order that we may also share in his glory.[202]

It is great that Paul uses the intimate 'Abba' or 'Daddy' to describe this new relationship. As a father, I have loved the times when you and Joseph used to snuggle up in a cuddle as I would read you a bedtime story, or when you would run into my arms when I came home, or when you would just excitedly tell me about something you were doing.

Now that you are older, although the nature of those interactions may change, I still enjoy the occasional hug, or hearing all about your plans and things you are achieving, or watching you grow and turn into a lovely young woman. You are, and always will be, my very special child. And I'm sure that is how God feels about you a hundred times over.

---

201 Galatians 4:6–7.

202 Romans 8:15–17.

11

BECOMING

*Whoever wants to be my disciple must deny themselves
and take up their cross and follow me.*

- Mark 8:34

As I have reflected on the nature of becoming like a little child, I have wondered too how we can actually put that into practice. My dearest Esther, I hope you will indulge me a little if I offer some fatherly advice on how to cultivate this nature. I would like to suggest a routine that we could do on a daily, or perhaps weekly, basis, to help us to follow Jesus's call to become like a little child. The suggestions below are all things I have found helpful over the years in my walk with God, although I haven't necessarily combined them all in this way. I hope you too will find them helpful as a means of drawing closer to Jesus.

In offering these suggestions, I recognise that we are all different and therefore find different approaches helpful. We also change over time. Things that are helpful at one stage of life may seem less so at another. So, while I can offer some ideas, I would encourage you to experiment, to discover your own rhythms and practices, to find the things that are most helpful to you in seeking to follow Jesus and become like a little child.

Going back to chapter 2, on vulnerability, you will remember we considered three basic requirements a newborn baby needs to survive: nutrition, hygiene, and safety. I will use these three as a structure for coming to God in humility as a child, relating these to practices of feeding, cleansing, and dressing. To these, I will add the fourth basic requirement of love, here expressed as resting.

1. Cleansing

As a baby relies on her parents to clean and change her, we come to God, acknowledging our brokenness, contamination, sin, and suffering, and ask the Holy One to make us clean.

There are a number of ways I have found to do this. The most simple is to use the prayer of the tax collector: 'God, have mercy on me, a sinner'.[203] Or in a slight extension of this, 'Lord Jesus Christ, Son of God, have mercy on me, a sinner'. I often recite this in the shower, allowing the water to wash me clean and at the same time imagining God making me clean inside. It can be helpful just to quietly say it over and over again, acknowledging our vulnerability before God and inviting God to have mercy on us.

Another helpful approach is to say one of the prayers of confession from a prayer book. Or to read all or part of Psalm 51 or Psalm 139. 'Search me, O God, and know my heart; test me and know my anxious thoughts. See if there is any offensive way in me, and lead me in the way everlasting.'[204]

Confession seems to me to be more than just repeating a list of misdemeanours and asking God to forgive each one. Rather, it is acknowledging our brokenness and vulnerability and accepting that we are not and cannot be truly holy. Sometimes we will have specific

---

[203]   Luke 18:13.
[204]   Psalm 139:23–24.

sins we need to confess. At other times, the simple ritual of saying a prayer of confession can be cleansing in its own right.

Meditation

Another technique I have tried is to use a short meditation exercise. Richard Foster, in *Celebration of discipline,* suggests two particularly helpful exercises: 'palms down, palms up' and 'inhale, exhale'.[205] In each of these, we use simple physical symbols to help us give our hurts and sin to God and receive in return the cleansing and healing of the Holy Spirit. You can use these to lay before God your sin, the things you know you have done wrong, but also the hurts you have received from others, the pains you feel, and the worries that crowd into your life. In return, God takes all that and lets us feel once again clean, whole, and healthy.

Palms Down, Palms Up

Begin by placing your palms down as a symbolic indication of your desire to turn over any concerns you may have to God. Inwardly you may pray, 'Lord, I give to you my anger toward Joe. I release my fear of my piano performance this evening. I surrender my anxiety over not getting my assignment completed ...' Whatever it is that weighs on your mind or is a concern to you, release it with your palms down. After several moments of surrender, turn your palms up as a symbol of your desire to receive from God. You may pray silently, 'Lord, I receive your divine love for Joe, I receive your peace for my exam this morning, your patience, your joy ...'

Inhale, Exhale

In this exercise you concentrate on your breathing as a means of centring yourself on God. Seat yourself comfortably, and quietly become aware of your breathing. Inhale deeply, filling your lungs;

---

[205] R. Foster. *Celebration of discipline.* Sevenoaks: Hodder & Stoughton, 1980, 24–25

then exhale slowly. Do this several times. Then with each breath pray inwardly, 'Lord, I exhale my fear over my maths exam, I inhale your peace. I exhale my spiritual apathy, I inhale your light and life …'

As with the palms down, palms up exercise, use this exercise to release your pain, worries, and sin to God and be filled instead with God's life-giving Spirit.

2. Feeding

Our primary source of spiritual nutrition is God's Word. We need to immerse ourselves in the Bible. This requires regular reading, study, and meditation, both on our own and with others. I personally have found it helpful to read a short passage of the Bible each morning before praying. Sometimes I have used Bible reading notes to help reflect on that; at other times I have used more contemplative approaches.

While that provides a regular daily exercise for me, I also like to branch out and engage with the Bible in different ways. Being someone who works very verbally and who enjoys intellectual challenges, I like to spend time studying the Bible – perhaps working through a particular book with the aid of a commentary, or picking up on different themes and pursuing my own study, or reading books that others have written.

Biblical meditation

Intellectual study of the Bible only goes so far, though. We really need to engage with God's Word on a deeper level as well, using our bodies, hearts, and souls as well as our minds to allow the Divine to speak.

The best way I have found to do this is through Biblical meditation, and the related exercises of *lectio divina* and imaginative prayer.

Lectio divina

The practice of *lectio divina*, from the Benedictine tradition, is a well-established approach to engaging directly with God's Word.[206] There are four stages involved:

1. *Lectio.* Start by slowly reading a passage of the Bible, then rereading it slowly, sometimes three or four times, until a particular word, phrase, or concept seems to draw your attention.
2. *Meditatio.* Spend time repeating and dwelling on that word or phrase, exploring it, seeking the meaning in it for you, for us. Observe the thoughts and feelings that arise in response to the word, and allow these to probe your attitudes, beliefs, and emotions.
3. *Oratio.* In response to that word, talk with God, not being afraid to express your deepest thoughts, feelings, hopes, and fears. You can do this silently or out loud, or use different media, such as journaling, art, music, or movement.
4. *Contemplatio.* Having expressed yourself, you finally become still, resting in the Holy One's presence, letting go of your thoughts and feelings, and just being with the God who loves you.

Imaginative prayer

In imaginative prayer, we are using our imaginations to help us enter a place where God can talk with us. This is prayer, not so much as an exercise in talking to God (although it can be a very helpful way of presenting our thoughts, concerns, and feelings to God), but rather as listening and feeding.

---

[206] A helpful exploration of the meaning and practice of *lectio divina* can be found in M. Basil Pennington. 'A Christian way to transformation'. *Spirituality Today.* 1983; 35(3): 220–229.

In imaginative prayer, we use our imaginations to enter into a story from the Bible, becoming a participant and, through that, being open to an encounter with the living God. The basic approach can be applied to almost any story from the gospels, and many other stories in the Bible.

I start these exercises by carefully reading, once or twice, the passage in question. I then close my Bible and spend some time stilling myself before working through the story again, imagining myself within it. I shall describe two examples that I have used several times.

The road to Emmaus

For this exercise, I imagine myself accompanying the two disciples as they walk along the road to Emmaus.[207] I imagine walking along a quiet, dusty road in the late afternoon, experiencing the rural sights and sounds. I listen to the disciples discussing the events of Holy Week, culminating in Jesus's death, and their puzzlement over the report of the women. I try to imagine what it must have been like at that point, not knowing or understanding the end of the story.

In my imagination, I then join in the conversation and express things that I find difficult – perhaps throwing in questions that I am struggling with, difficult situations I have been facing, or concerns that I have. I use this opportunity to be frank and open about things that are real issues to me now.

Next, I imagine Jesus coming up and walking alongside us. At this point, I find it easier to imagine myself knowing it is Jesus, but with the two disciples not knowing. I listen to Jesus talking with the disciples, and imagine how he might explain what had happened. After a while, Jesus turns to me, and the two of us drop behind the other two. Jesus asks me what I have been discussing with the other two. Sometimes I find this can be a very powerful moment, as I

---

[207] Luke 24:13–32.

express to Jesus the reality of my own struggles. It is not a time to hold back – Jesus, walking beside me, can take it all.

Once I have expressed what is on my heart, I am quiet. In my imagination, I continue to walk along the road beside Jesus. I allow him to speak. Often I find he is silent, and I am not able to imagine what he might be saying. In those times, I simply try to continue imagining myself walking and not worry about the silence. At other times, I do get a sense of Jesus saying something to me, and I walk with that word.

To finish the meditation, I imagine the four of us arriving at a village. The disciples invite Jesus and me to join them for a meal. We sit down, and I imagine Jesus blessing the bread and wine, the disciples' recognition of him, and his gentle disappearance, leaving the three of us sitting quietly, just being still for a time.

Children coming to Jesus

I have used this meditation both as a way of coming to Jesus myself and as a way of bringing to him others for whom I want to pray, in which case I imagine them as the ones sitting on the wall and going over to Jesus. Start by reading the story of the children coming to Jesus.[208]

Imagine yourself in a town setting in Palestine at the time of Jesus. You notice a big crowd of people gathered in an open square. Right in the middle, Jesus is talking with some Pharisees. You climb up and sit on a wall, from which you can see what is happening. You notice some of the women trying to go up to Jesus with their little children, but the disciples who are standing there with him tell them to go away and not to bother him while he is busy talking. Jesus turns to his disciples crossly and tells them not to stop the children coming to him, because the kingdom of God belongs to them. Several mothers with their young children go forward, and Jesus puts his hands on them and prays for them.

---

[208]   Matthew 19:13–15.

Then Jesus looks up and sees you sitting on the wall. He calls you: 'Esther, come over here.' You get up and push through the crowd to get to him. When you get there, he says, 'Why don't we go for a walk, away from all these people?' Jesus puts his arm around your shoulder, and the two of you walk off, away from the crowd.

As you walk, let him talk to you. Try to listen to what he might be saying. Feel free to talk to him about anything you want to – it may be to thank him for something, tell him about what you're doing, or pour out your feelings or worries.

Once you feel you have had a chance to talk and to listen, turn and thank him, then imagine yourself walking back to the present.

3. Resting

Some of the most rewarding times I found in being your parent, dear Esther, were those moments when I would sit with you for a cuddle just after you had been changed and fed. I suspect God feels the same about us and wants us just to rest with him at times. In one sense, this is straightforward, and flows naturally from the meditation exercises described above. Having spent time in confession, reading, meditation, or prayer, we just rest quietly in God's presence. There is no agenda here, other than to be with God.

However, this resting is not something we necessarily find easy. You will find this more and more as you go through work and university – there will always be things to do. Our busyness impinges on this time with God, and it can feel unjustified taking time out of our schedules. I have found, though, that the busier I am, the more important it is to take time just to be still.

There are lots of ways you can do this, and plenty of opportunities for being still. The key is to look for these opportunities and take them as they arise. They can be small moments, such as pausing for a minute before starting a piece of work, or more substantial times set aside.

Getting outside into God's creation can help. Just a simple walk down the garden each evening, or taking our dog Neo for a walk can be a way of resting with God. For me, this naturally flows into praise: spending time with God, resting in presence of the Divine. Particularly where we can be aware of creation around us, this provides the setting for worshipping God, who made us, who loves us, and who made this wonderful world in which we live. Music can help: playing, singing, or listening to worship songs – indeed to any beautiful music. In allowing our creativity to express itself, we are worshipping the ultimate Creator of all things.

I think it is also helpful to set aside more specific times to be silent with God. Taking out a day, or half a day, each year to spend with God is incredibly valuable, and something I have tried to build into my life.

You could use such times to look back over the past year, reflecting on how you have developed – particularly in terms of the aspects of spiritual development outlined in chapter 8. How have you grown in your awareness of yourself (body, mind, heart, and soul), of God, of others, and of creation? Then look forward, listening to God as you do so. In what ways does God want you to develop over the coming year – in relation to yourself, in relation to God, in relation to other people, and in relation to the world around us?

4. Dressing

For this final aspect of coming before God as a child, I want to draw on Paul's description of the armour of God:

> Finally, be strong in the Lord and in his mighty
> power. Put on the full armour of God, so that you

can take your stand against the devil's schemes.
For our struggle is not against flesh and blood, but
against the rulers, against the authorities, against the
powers of this dark world and against the spiritual
forces of evil in the heavenly realms. Therefore put
on the full armour of God, so that when the day of
evil comes, you may be able to stand your ground,
and after you have done everything, to stand. Stand
firm then, with the belt of truth buckled around
your waist, with the breastplate of righteousness in
place, and with your feet fitted with the readiness
that comes from the gospel of peace. In addition to
all this, take up the shield of faith, with which you
can extinguish all the flaming arrows of the evil
one. Take the helmet of salvation and the sword of
the Spirit, which is the word of God.[209]

An exercise which I have found useful is to imagine yourself
putting on this armour, praying through each element as you put it on.

Put on the belt of truth around your waist. Ask God to make you
truthful in all your thoughts, words, and deeds. Confess any lies,
half-truths, or hypocrisy in your life. Commit to striving for truth
in all you do.

Put on a breastplate of righteousness. Ask that your heart will be
solely devoted to seeking first God's kingdom and his righteousness.
Ask God to help you live in right relationship with him and with
other people – in purity of thought, word, and deed. Reflect on
Paul's exhortation: 'Whatever is true, whatever is noble, whatever is
right, whatever is pure, whatever is lovely, whatever is admirable – if
anything is excellent or praiseworthy – think about such things.'[210]

---

[209] Ephesians 6:10–17.
[210] Philippians 4:8.

Put on the shoes of the readiness that comes from the gospel of peace.
Commit yourself to spreading Jesus's good news of peace. Ask God
to give you courage to live and speak for him. Ask him to lead you
to places, people, and situations where you can bring the blessings
of God's kingdom.

Take up the shield of faith. Recognise your vulnerability and ask
for God's protection in all you come across. Ask him to help you
trust him. If you are feeling particularly vulnerable or under attack,
think of God's promises that may help you to counter these attacks.

Put on the helmet of salvation. Thank God for his salvation,
through which you have been set free to be the person God created
you to be. Ask God to protect your mind from all unwanted thoughts
and any sense of unworthiness, anxiety, or hopelessness.

Take up the sword of the spirit. Reflect on anything you have
read from God's Word recently. Ask God to help you remember his
Word and use it in the situations you might face today. Ask him
to give you words to say to others that will bring comfort, healing,
hope, and peace.

Disciplines of grace

Esther, my dear child, in this chapter I have outlined some
ways in which you and I can take steps towards becoming like
a little child. I have done so with some caution though. Just as a
young infant does not come into the world through her own effort,
nor struggle to grow and develop through an act of will, so, for us,
becoming a child in the way Jesus intended is not something we can
achieve through our own effort.

Becoming a child is a gift from God; it stems from God's grace.
The challenge for us is not to strive to obey all the rules, practice
all the right disciplines, and so somehow convince God that we are
really like children. Rather it is to respond to God's invitation and

accept God's grace. In particular, it is to recognise that God loves us unconditionally, just as a father loves his child, and even more so. You, my dear Esther, are God's beloved child.

From that starting point, however, I believe there are things that you and I can do to cultivate that childlike spirit that Jesus calls us to. In response to God's grace, and in anticipation of God's kingdom of peace, we can live as children, and so grow and develop to become the children that God sees in us.

This, in time, will enable you to grow deeper into God's love and to develop into the person God made you to be. As you practice these disciplines of grace, God will work in you to develop your character. One consequence is that you are likely to find yourself wanting to go even further.

In his first letter, the apostle Peter encourages his readers 'like newborn babies [to] crave pure spiritual milk, so that by it you may grow up in your salvation.'[211] He wants his readers to grow to maturity through craving spiritual nourishment.

The writer to the Hebrews takes this even further: 'Anyone who lives on milk, being still an infant, is not acquainted with the teaching about righteousness. But solid food is for the mature, who by constant use have trained themselves to distinguish good from evil.'[212]

As you continue in your journey of faith, I would encourage you to make a habit of spending time with God, of drawing on this nourishment. In doing so, you can grow to maturity, becoming even more the beautiful person God made you to be. As you do so, I am sure that you will come to see more of God's kingdom and all that that means.

---

[211] 1 Peter 2:2.

[212] Hebrews 5:13–14.

12

DESTINY

I pray that the eyes of your heart may be enlightened in order that you may know the hope to which he has called you, the riches of his glorious inheritance in his holy people, and his incomparably great power for us who believe.

- Ephesians 1:18.19

Through this book I have explored my understanding of what it might mean to become like a little child, drawing on my understanding of child development. In this, my dear Esther, you have been perhaps my greatest teacher. What I have put down in this book draws largely on what you have given me – the gift of being your father. Now, as you move into your adult life, I am full of joy and pride in all you have given me, in hope for what you will be, and above all, in love for you, my daughter.

The kingdom of heaven

I want to turn finally to look at where this is leading, and to consider what the kingdom of heaven is and what it might mean to enter it. Jesus's exhortation to change and become like little children was linked to a purpose. In doing so, he was suggesting that we would enter the kingdom of heaven.[213] Similarly, his challenge to Nicodemus was that, by being born again, he would see the kingdom of God.[214]

So, if we choose to change, to be born again and become like little children, what is it that we will be entering or seeing or receiving?

Jesus spoke a lot about the kingdom of God, or the kingdom of heaven, and it seems that he used these two phrases interchangeably. A lot of his parables and his teaching were about this kingdom. Indeed, it would appear that his primary purpose was to proclaim the 'good news of the kingdom'.[215]

The more I think about this, the more convinced I am that Jesus was not talking about some future, distant place called heaven where we might go when we die. Rather, I think he was talking about something very real, very present, here and now.

As Jesus started out his ministry, he did so echoing John's words:

Repent, for the kingdom of heaven is near.[216]

Jesus went into Galilee, proclaiming the good news of God. 'The time has come,' he said. 'The kingdom of God is near.'[217]

When a teacher of the law seemed to grasp Jesus's message that the most important commandments were to love God and to love your neighbour, he told the man, 'You are not far from the kingdom of God.'[218] He told his disciples to proclaim that the kingdom of God was near.[219]

---

[213] Matthew 18:3.

[214] John 3:3.

[215] Mathew 4:23; 9:35; Luke 8:1.

[216] Matthew 3:2; 4:17.

[217] Mark 1:15.

[218] Mark 12:34.

[219] Luke 10:9.

When people wanted to follow him, but only at a later date, Jesus seemed to suggest some urgency to service in the kingdom of God:

> He said to another man, 'Follow me.' But the man replied, 'Lord, first let me go and bury my father.' Jesus said to him, 'Let the dead bury their own dead, but you go and proclaim the kingdom of God.'
>
> Still another said, 'I will follow you, Lord; but first let me go back and say good-bye to my family.' Jesus replied, 'No-one who puts his hand to the plough and looks back is fit for service in the kingdom of God.'[220]

When Jesus was asked specifically when the kingdom of God would come, he replied, 'The kingdom of God does not come with your careful observation, nor will people say, "Here it is," or "there it is," because the kingdom of God is within you.'[221]

It seems to me that the implication of all these verses is that Jesus considered the kingdom of heaven to be something that he was inaugurating at that time. When he read from the scroll of the prophet Isaiah, he concluded his reading by saying, 'Today this scripture is fulfilled in your hearing.'[222] So, by encouraging his followers to be born again and become like little children, Jesus was inviting them to enter his kingdom of heaven right there and then.

An in-between time

While Jesus initiated his kingdom 2,000 years ago in Galilee, and while this kingdom is something which I believe we can be part

---

[220] Luke 9:59–62.

[221] Luke 17:20–21.

[222] Luke 4:21.

of right now, it is also clear to me that this kingdom of heaven has not yet been fully established. We are living in an in-between time, in which we may see aspects of God's kingdom but we certainly don't see it in all its fullness. Children continue to get abused; people continue to use violence to promote their causes; the rich get richer at the expense of those who are poor, vulnerable, and exploited; people continue to get sick, suffer, and die; and our world remains troubled and damaged.

And yet we can look forward to a time when God's kingdom will come in all its fullness, and the whole of creation will be restored and reconciled to God.

A new heaven and a new earth

I have found myself increasingly inspired by all I read about in the Bible in relation to God's kingdom, and to a time when God will create a new heaven and a new earth. It seems to me that this will not be in the sense of destroying this earth and all we know, but rather completely transforming it into all it was intended to be. In this new kingdom, we too will be restored and made new – body, mind, heart, and soul. We will be brought into a right relationship with God, with ourselves, with others, and with creation. In this new kingdom, all sin, suffering, and injustice will be overturned and replaced with wholeness, peace, and joy.

In his second letter, Peter emphasises that, 'in keeping with [God's] promise we are looking forward to a new heaven and a new earth, where righteousness dwells.'[223]

Isaiah provides a powerful picture of what this new heaven and earth will look like:

> Never again will there be in it
> an infant who lives but a few days,

---

[223] 2 Peter 3:13.

or an old man who does not live out his years ...
They will build houses and dwell in them;
they will plant vineyards and eat their fruit ...
They will not labour in vain,
nor will they bear children doomed to misfortune;
for they will be a people blessed by the LORD,
they and their descendants with them.[224]

What an incredible hope! That to me sounds very real and earthy – not some distant, ethereal abode in the sky. Rather, we will build houses, plant, eat, work, create, and have children. In this kingdom, all of creation will be restored, to the extent that the wolf and the lamb will feed together.[225]

And there will be no more war:

> He will judge between many peoples and will settle
> disputes for strong nations far and wide. They
> will beat their swords into ploughshares and their
> spears into pruning hooks. Nation will not take up
> sword against nation, nor will they train for war
> anymore.[226]

This vision of a world restored is picked up also by John in his revelation of a new heaven and a new earth:

> And I heard a loud voice from the throne saying,
> 'Look! God's dwelling place is now among the
> people, and he will dwell with them. They will be
> his people, and God himself will be with them and
> be their God. He will wipe every tear from their
> eyes. There will be no more death or mourning or

---

[224] Isaiah 65:20–23.
[225] Isaiah 65:25.
[226] Micah 4:3.

crying or pain, for the old order of things has passed away.'[227]

In my work, when I spend time with children who have been abused, or with families whose baby has died, or with parents who are struggling to bring up a severely disabled child, that vision of God's kingdom is largely what keeps me going. It is something I look forward to with hope, and I long for that day when there will be no more death or mourning or crying or pain. I look forward to the day when heaven and earth come together, when God's dwelling place will be among his people. The Bible is clear that we are not there yet, but that this is a certainty in which we can hope.

The whole story of the Bible presents the good news of God's kingdom, and it ends with the restoration of creation as God intended it to be.

The last chapter of Revelation presents a picture of this new creation, at the very centre of which is the river of the water of life, flowing from the throne of God: 'On each side of the river stood the tree of life, bearing twelve crops of fruit, yielding its fruit every month. And the leaves of the tree are for the healing of the nations. No longer will there be any curse.'[228]

That tree of life, which was barred to humankind following the fall, will be there, bearing fruit for all, and bringing healing to all people and to all of creation. The curse that was put in place in Genesis chapter 3 will be no more. What an incredible thought. It is because of this that I long, with John, for Jesus's coming: 'He who testifies to these things says, "Yes, I am coming soon." Amen. Come, Lord Jesus.'[229]

---

227 Revelation 21:3–4.
228 Revelation 22:2–3.
229 Revelation 22:20.

Seeking God's kingdom

My dear Esther, for nineteen years you have lived with me, your father. Over this time I have watched you grow and develop into a beautiful young woman. Now, as you set off on a new stage in your journey, I pray that you will discover more and more what it means, not to leave your childhood behind, but to hold on to that childhood, and through that to enter more fully into God's wonderful kingdom, here and now.

Jesus taught his disciples to pray, 'Your kingdom come, your will be done on earth as it is in heaven'.[230] He wanted them and us to pray for God's kingdom to come. We too can pray that the fullness of God's kingdom that we have just explored will become more and more real here and now, in our lives and, through us, in the world around us. We pray that people will be healed, that there will be an end to suffering, and that premature deaths will be prevented. We pray for an end to the injustice and oppression that affects so many; for violence, greed, and exploitation to be crushed; for people to care for this world and work for its good.

This, though, is a dangerous prayer that will lead to action. First and foremost, it will lead to action on our parts. We need to take seriously the challenges Jesus put to his disciples in following him.

Loving God

First, each of us seeks to love God with all our heart, and with all our soul, and with all our mind, and with all our strength. We have seen what shape that might take as every part of our being is fulfilled in loving God. This means that we will spend time with God. It means that other gods will be pushed aside. It means that we will go against the tide of popular ambition and culture, not seeking the wealth, comfort, position, or pleasure that ultimately

---

[230] Matthew 6:10.

fails to fill that gap in who we were created to be. Rather, we will celebrate who we are in Christ, enjoying the creativity, exploration, and relationship that make up our being. In loving God, we are set free to find our true identities.

My precious daughter, as you move away from home through university and beyond, I believe you will discover more and more of who you are, created as a child of God.

You will discover something more of your creativity, of the gifts God has given you. You will use your mind to learn, to explore, and to discover. You will find new ways to celebrate and enjoy the goodness of this world. And you will form exciting new relationships with others.

I pray that you will make the most of all these opportunities. And above all, I pray that you will come to love God more and more as the one who truly loves you:

> I pray that you, being rooted and established in love, may have power, together with all the saints, to grasp how wide and long and high and deep is the love of Christ, and to know this love that surpasses knowledge – that you may be filled to the measure of all the fullness of God.[231]

Loving others

Second, we will seek to love our neighbours as ourselves. We will strive for justice and extend compassion to those in need. We will be there for others.

In doing so, we will make ourselves vulnerable. We won't turn away from those who are suffering. But that will hurt. John Ortberg has expressed it powerfully:

---

[231] Ephesians 3:17–19.

In a contagious world, we learn to keep our distance. If we get too close to those who are suffering we might get infected by their pain. It may not be convenient or comfortable. But only when you get close enough to catch their hurt will they be close enough to catch your love.[232]

As you go through your life, my daughter, I am sure you will come across troubling and difficult situations. You may well experience some of that pain. But, in doing so, you are helping to bring God's kingdom here on earth. Through your tears, you will be lifting those people and situations up to your heavenly Father, with that cry for God's kingdom to come on earth, as it is in heaven.

Entering God's kingdom

I think there is something very important in putting the two great commandments in the order they come: first, we love God; then we express that in loving our neighbours. If we try to love our neighbours like that in our own strength, we will fail; we run the danger of becoming burned out. We long for God's kingdom of peace and wholeness, but we can never bring that about in our own strength. This kingdom is not some utopian ideal to be achieved through human endeavour. It is only when we are, like children, in a right relationship with God, our Father and Creator, that we can have the security and strength to reach out to others with his love.

As we do so, first we, then through us others, and ultimately the whole of creation can come to experience what it means to enter God's amazing kingdom:

The creation waits in eager expectation for the sons of God to be revealed. For the creation was

---

[232]   J. Ortberg. *Love beyond reason*. Zondervan: Grand Rapids, MI, 1980, 56.

subjected to frustration, not by its own choice, but by the will of the one who subjected it, in hope that the creation itself will be liberated from its bondage to decay and brought into the glorious freedom of the children of God.[233]

---

[233]   Romans 8:19–21.

ABOUT THE AUTHOR

Peter Sidebotham is an associate professor of child health at Warwick Medical School. He is an academic consultant paediatrician, specialising in child development, care of disabled children, child protection work, and support for bereaved families.

He undertakes teaching and research in a number of fields, particularly related to child maltreatment and child death review. He is recognised nationally and internationally as a leader in these fields. He has published extensively, with a large number of academic papers in peer-reviewed journals, an edited book, and several book chapters and research reports. He is a co-editor of the scientific journal *Child Abuse Review*.

Peter has two grown-up children. He lives in Coventry, UK, where he is an active member of an Anglican church. He has had many years' experience of helping with and leading children and youth work in the Church and other Christian settings.